Eight Lectures on
India's Economic Reforms

Eight Lectures on
India's Economic Reforms

T. N. Srinivasan

OXFORD
UNIVERSITY PRESS

OXFORD

UNIVERSITY PRESS

YMCA Library Building, Jai Singh Road, New Delhi 110001

Oxford University Press is a department of the University of Oxford. It furthers the
University's objective of excellence in research, scholarship, and education
by publishing worldwide in

Oxford   New York

Athens   Auckland   Bangkok   Bogota   Buenos Aires   Calcutta
Cape Town   Chennai   Dar es Salaam   Delhi   Florence   Hong Kong   Istanbul
Karachi   Kuala Lumpur   Madrid   Melbourne   Mexico City   Mumbai
Nairobi   Paris   Sao Paolo   Singapore   Taipei   Tokyo   Toronto   Warsaw

with associated companies in   Berlin   Ibadan
Oxford is a registered trade mark of Oxford University Press
in the UK and in certain other countries

Published in India
By Oxford University Press, New Delhi

ISBN 019 565282 7

Typeset in Galliard BT
by InoSoft Systems, New Delhi 110 092
Printed at Rashtriya Printers, Delhi 110 032
Published by Manzar Khan, Oxford University Press
YMCA Library Building, Jai Singh Road, New Delhi 110 001

Contents

List of Abbreviations

ADM	anti-dumping
ADR	American Depository Receipts
BIFR	Bureau for Industrial and Financial Restructuring
BOP	Balance of Payments
BOT	Build Operate Transfer
CRAR	Capital to Risk-weighted Asset Ratio
DOT	Department of Telecommunications
DPAP	Drought Prone Areas Programme
DPEP	District Primary Education Programme
DWCRA	Development of Women and Children in Rural Areas
EAS	Employment Assurance Scheme
FDI	Foreign Direct Investment
FIIs	Foreign Institutional Investors
FIPB	Foreign Investment Promotion Board
GATS	General Agreement on Trade in Services
GDP	Gross Domestic Product
GDR	Global Depository Receipts
ICDS	Integrated Child Development Services
IEG	Institute of Economic Growth
IRD	Integrated Rural Development
IRDP	Integrated Rural Development Programme
ISEC	Institute for Social and Economic Change
JRY	Jawahar Rozgar Yojna
LRS	Labour Reserve Service
MFN	Most Favoured Nation
MIDS	Madras Institute for Development Studies
NBFI	Non Bank Financial Institutions
NDP	Net Domestic Product
NPA	Non Performing Assets

NRI	Non Resident Indians
NTPC	National Thermal Power Corporation
OGL	Open General License
PDS	Public Distribution System
PMO	Prime Minister's Office
PSEs	Public Sector Enterprises
PSUs	Public Sector Undertakings
PTAs	Preferential Trade Agreements
PW	Public Works
QR	Quantitative Restrictions
SAPTA	South Asian Preferential Trade Agreement
SEBI	Security and Exchanges Board of India
SERC	State Electricity Regulatory Commission
TAMP	Tariff Authority for Major Ports
TFP	Total Factor Productivity
TIFR	Tata Institute of Fundamental Research
TRAI	Telecommunications Regulatory Authority of India
TRYSEMS	Training of Youth and Self-employment Programmes
UNDP	United Nations Development Programme
VAT	Value Added Tax
WTO	World Trade Organization

Preface

I was indeed greatly honoured and privileged to be the first holder of the endowment professorship established by the Institute for Social and Economic Change (ISEC), Bangalore in memory of its founder, Dr V.K.R.V. Rao. I thank Dr P.V. Shenoi, its former Director, and the Governing Board for bestowing this honour on me. I spent March and July 1998 at the Institute and very much enjoyed my stay in the peaceful, green and lovely campus. I wish to thank Dr P.V. Shenoi, the faculty and staff of ISEC and the Registrars, Dr S.N. Sangita and Dr V. Reddy, for their ever courteous and generous hospitality during my stay.

My association with Dr Rao dates back to 1962–3 when I spent a year at the Institute of Economic Growth (IEG) in Delhi, another of India's great research institutions in economics founded by him. During my tenure at the Indian Statistical Institute (ISI), Delhi during the sixties and seventies, we met occasionally in Delhi and Bangalore. I fondly remember the warm hospitality of Dr and Mrs Rao whenever I visited their homes. Dr Rao, a distinguished economist and statesman, was above all, an institution builder. In all three institutions he built, namely, the Delhi School of Economics, IEG and ISEC, Dr Rao emphasized the inter-relationships among all social sciences by having talented sociologists, social anthropologists, and political scientists as well as economists from all parts of India on the faculty.

I had the privilege to personally know another great scholar–institution builder, Professor P.C. Mahalanobis of the ISI. Through my old classmates at Loyola College, Madras, who went on to work as mathematicians at another great institution, the Tata Institute of Fundamental Research (TIFR) I came to know of its guiding spirit Dr Homi Bhabha. Each of these three towering personalities left their indelible and unique marks, not only, as is to be expected, on the research being pursued at these institutions but also on the architecture and their styles of functioning. All three believed in going beyond their own discipline in fostering research in related disciplines. I hope that someday a scholar will write a comparative biography of these three titans and the institutions they created.

During my first visit in March 1998, Dr Shenoi wanted me to lecture both at the ISEC and also at her sister research institutes in South India, namely, the Administrative Staff College at Hyderabad, the Centre for Development Studies at Thiruvananthapuram, the Centre for Economic and Social Studies at Hyderabad, and the Madras Institute for Development Studies (MIDS) at Chennai. I also lectured at the Institute of Development Studies at the University of Mysore. The lecture I delivered under the auspices of the ISEC in Bangalore and subsequently at Hyderabad, Mysore, and Thiruvananthapuram has been published in the January–June 1999 issue of ISEC's journal, *Journal of Social and Economic Development,* vol. II, no. 1, with the title 'WTO and the Developing Countries'. The lecture I delivered at MIDS, Madras has already appeared in the July–December 1998 issue of their journal, *Review of Development & Change,* vol. III, no. 2, with the title 'Democracy, Markets, Governance and Development'.

During my second visit to the ISEC in July 1998, Dr Shenoi wanted me to take stock of the state of economic reforms in India. I gave eight lectures in all. While each of the lectures addresses reforms in different sectors of the economy, I have tried to set the current situation in a historical context. This is because of my firm belief that without understanding the pre-independence origins of our development strategy until the 1991 reforms and the early political consensus in its favour, it is difficult to understand not only what motivated Prime Minister Narasimha Rao and Finance Minister Dr Manmohan Singh to initiate *systemic* reforms in July 1991 but also why they were delayed until that time, and why there still is some serious resistance to reviving, deepening, and extending the reforms. While learning about the history is certainly helpful in understanding the present, one would hope that Karl Marx would be proved wrong in yet another of his assertions (in the Eighteenth

Brumiere) that 'history repeats itself, once as a tragedy, and then as a farce'.

Eradication of mass poverty was the laudable and overarching objective of our leaders and thinkers, including Dadabhai Naoroji, Mahatma Gandhi, and Pandit Nehru. It was also the goal of the businessmen who published their *Bombay Plan* (Thakurdas *et al.* 1944) and the labour leaders who also published their own *People's Plan* (Bannerjee *et al.* 1944) in the same year, not to mention our post-independence governments. More than five decades after independence we are, alas, nowhere near achieving this objective. But if it is to be achieved in a not too distant future and India is to gain its rightful place as a self reliant and vibrant economy in the world, it is absolutely essential that our future leaders have the courage and wisdom to move boldly across several fronts in extending and accelerating the reforms initiated by Dr Manmohan Singh.

I owe a deep debt of gratitude to the commentators at my lectures, M. Prahladachar, K.N. Ninan, R.S. Deshpande, M.J. Bhende, Hemlata Rao, A.S. Seetharamu, K.G. Gayathri, K.N. M. Raju, and M.R. Narayana as well as others who participated in the discussion following each lecture. I should also thank, in particular, Dr P.V. Shenoi, Dr G.V.K. Rao, Dr Abdul Aziz, Mr. Satish Chandran, Professor P.R. Brahmananda, Dr N.S. Iyengar, and Dr G. Thimmaiah who presided over the lectures and offered valuable comments. I am grateful to Subbiah Kannappan, Anne Krueger, Suresh Tendulkar, and A. Vaidyanathan who were kind enough to read the written version of the lectures and provide extensive comments which I have tried to incorporate. Last, but not least, I thank my secretary Louise Danishevsky, not only for producing readable versions from my virtually unreadable handwritten drafts, but also for bringing efficiency and order to my otherwise chaotic office.

I thank Dr Govinda Rao, who succeeded Dr P.V. Shenoi as the Director of ISEC, for his keen interest in having these lectures published. I spent several weeks during the summer of 1999 reusing them for publication, at the Center for Research on Economic Development and Policy Reform, Stanford University, following an invitation from its founder Director, Professor Krueger. I thank Professor Krueger for her warm hospitality and the intellectual stimulation from her colleagues at the Center.

As I was revising the lectures, the Election Commission announced the schedule for the general elections of September 1999. The National Democratic Alliance led by the Bharatiya Janata Party has since won an absolute majority and took office in October 1999. It has promised to acclerate reforms. I very much hope that these lectures will stimulate further discussion on our reforms among the political parties in power and in the opposition, as well as the public.

1

The Industrial Sector

Let me begin with a brief recapitulation of our industrial policy prior to the reforms of 1991. Industrialization, through import substitution and public sector production with emphasis on heavy industry, has been a very important objective of our planning for development, at least since Sir M. Visveswaraya published his *Planned Economy for India* in Bangalore in 1934. He asserted that 'India cannot prosper except through industrialization [which] has to be organized, planned and worked for ... India may be an industrially developed country or it may be a market for manufactured goods from outside and not both' (Visveswaraya 1934, pp. 351–3). The National Planning Committee of the Indian National Congress by Pandit Jawaharlal Nehru argued in 1938 that

the problems of poverty and unemployment, of national defense and of economic regeneration in general cannot be solved without industrialization. [Nehru 1946, p. 401]

The three fundamental requirements of India, if she is to develop industrially and otherwise, are: a heavy engineering and machine-making industry, scientific research institutes, and electric power. These must be the foundations of all planning. [ibid, p. 416]

Thus even the enthusiastic advocates for cottage and small-scale industries recognize that big-scale industry is, to a certain extent, necessary and inevitable; only they would like to limit it as far as possible ... in the context of the modern world, no country can be politically and economically independent, even within the framework of international interdependence, unless it is highly industrialized and has developed its power resources to the utmost. Nor can it achieve or maintain high standards of living and liquidate poverty without the aid of modern technology in almost every sphere of life . . . . An attempt to build up a country's economy largely on the basis of cottage and small-scale industries is doomed to failure. It will not solve the basic problems of the country or maintain freedom, nor will it fit in with the world framework, except as a colonial appendage. [ibid, p. 413]

Other pre-independence plans, including the *Bombay Plan* (Thakurdas *et al.* 1944) of industrialists and the *People's Plan* of the Indian Federation of Labour (Banerjee *et al.* 1944), also emphasized industrialization.

In the post-independence period, even prior to the establishment of the Planning Commission in 1950, the Industrial Policy Resolution of 1948 (later amended and elaborated in 1956) had set the broad outlines of our industrial development strategy by distinguishing industries according to the end use of their outputs (capital, intermediate, and consumer goods), their ownership (public, cooperative, private, and joint) and their size or technology (cottage, village, small-scale, and organized). In particular, an important distinction was made among industries to be developed exclusively by the public sector, those reserved for the private sector, and those open to development by either or both sectors. Development of key industries, such as railways, telecommunications, and electricity generation, was assigned to the public sector. In addition, industries producing key industrial raw materials and equipment, such as steel, petroleum, and heavy machinery, including electric generators, were also assigned to the public sector.

The resolution was motivated by the idea that infrastructure and industries supplying key raw materials constituted what Lenin had described as the 'commanding heights' of an industrial battlefield. It was believed that by controlling these, the course of development of all industries, in the private and public sectors, could be made to follow in socially desirable directions. Moreover, instead of using taxation to generate revenue (for example, for investment in the public sector), the pricing of goods and services produced and supplied by the public sector could be used to generate a surplus. It was also believed that the choice of location of the public sector projects could be used to promote development of backward regions. Finally, the wages and working conditions of workers in the public sector were supposed to be a model for the private sector to follow.

The First Five Year Plan set the overall interventionist framework of policy, and the Second Plan (1956–61), authored by

Professor P. C. Mahalanobis, provided the analytical foundation for the development strategy that was pursued for the subsequent thirty five years.[1] It emphasized the development of heavy industries, import substitution across the board, and spearheaded a vast expansion of the public sector. The massive investment (relative to resources available for its financing) proposed in the Second Plan precipitated a macroeconomic and balance of payments crisis. In response, an elaborate system of controls (that was expanded in subsequent decades) was put in place to enforce the plans and their underlying development strategy.[2]

At its most expansive and inclusive, the system involved the following: *industrial licensing* under which the scale, technology, and location of any investment project other than relatively small ones were regulated and permission from the government was needed to expand, relocate, and change the output or input mixes of operating plants; the *exchange control system* which required exporters to surrender their foreign exchange earnings to the Reserve Bank of India at the official exchange rate, and allocated the exchange earnings to users through *import licensing; capital issues control* under which access to domestic equity markets and

---

[1] It is true that much of the investment in heavy industries took place in the sixties and seventies and, as such, subsequent plans did not emphasize these industries as much and somewhat deviated from the Mahalanobis strategy. But these deviations were more in the nature of *ad hoc* responses to emerging circumstances than the consequences of deliberate reconsideration of the strategy.

[2] The First Five Year Plan justified controls as essential for promoting rapid economic development by claiming:

Control and regulation of exports and imports, and in the case of certain commodities, state trading, are necessary not only from the point of view of utilizing to the best advantage the limited foreign exchange resources available but also for securing an allocation of productive resources of the country in line with targets defined in the Plan. . . .Viewed in the proper perspective, controls are but another aspect of the problem of incentives, for to the extent that controls limit the freedom of action on the part of certain classes, they provide correspondingly an incentive to certain others and the practical problem is to balance the loss of satisfaction in one case against the gain in the other. For one to ask for fuller employment and more rapid development and at the same time to object to controls is obviously to support two contradictory objectives. [Planning Commission, 1951, pp. 42–3, emphasis added]

debt finance was controlled; *price controls* (complete or partial) on some vital consumption goods (for example, foodgrains, sugar, vegetable oils) and critical inputs (for example, fertilizer, irrigation water, fuel); *made-to-measure* protection from import competition, granted to domestic producers in many 'priority' industries, including in particular the equipment producers.[3] The agricultural sector was insulated from world markets, subjected to land ceiling and tenancy legislation, and forced to sell part of the output at fixed prices, but it was also provided subsidies on irrigation, fertilizer, and electricity. Large commercial banks, which were nationalized in 1969, were subject to directed and selective credit controls, controls on deposit and lending rates, and in effect had to lend more than half of their loanable funds to government through the operation of reserve requirements of various kinds.

The controls taken together were far more restrictive than each of them individually. For example, grant of an industrial licence did not imply grant of a capital goods import licence so that the capacity licenced could not be operational if the intended imports were essential. Besides the crucial aspect of all the regulations is the uncertainty about their fair implementation because they were essentially *discretionary* rather than *rule-based* and *automatic*. Although some principles and priorities were to govern the exercise of these regulatory powers, these were largely non-operational for two reasons. First it was impossible, even in theory, to devise a set of principles or rules for all the myriad categories of regulations that were mutually consistent and in consonance with the multiple goals of the industrial policy framework, which in themselves were not entirely consistent. Second, the problem of translating whatever rules there were into operational decisions was one of Orwellian dimensions. The allocative mechanism was largely in the form of quantitative restrictions unrelated to market realities. A chaotic incentive

---

[3] There was the infamous 'indigenous clearance angle': any applicant for a licence to import equipment was required to advertise in the relevant trade journal his intention to apply for a licence. If *any* domestic manufacturer of a substitute responded saying that his product could meet the applicant's needs, the application was denied whether or not the product in fact met the needs and also whether its quality, cost, or time of delivery were comparable to that of the intended import.

structure and the unleashing of rapacious rent-seeking and political corruption were the inevitable outcomes. Indeed, the discretionary regulatory system instituted in the name of planning for national development instead became a cancer in the body politic.

Another dimension of the exercise of regulatory power was that it was *anticipatory* in nature—that is, the regulations were meant to *prevent* the occurence of any prospective deviation from the objectives of policy by firms or other regulated entities rather than to *punish* or cure any deviant behavior that actually occurred. While preventive, rather than curative, medicine is often preferable in health care systems, clearly it is not appropriate in industrial regulations. But in India a system of *curative* health care and *preventive* industrial regulations has been in existence since the 1950s!

The actual performance of the public sector enterprises (PSEs) has not conformed to the role envisaged. Far from promoting private sector development and channelling it in socially desirable directions, there has been poor performance in supplying key inputs in appropriate amounts and at the time and place where demands arise. There was low operational efficiency and a lack of resilience to change production patterns and technology. Commercial PSEs have been run on anything but commercial lines and, instead, very much as activities promoting the welfare of their employees as well as the bureaucrats and politicians who managed them. Also some PSEs were saddled with functions, other than main commercial ones, in the name of 'public interest'. Since the enterprises were not directly compensated for performing 'public interest' functions, their performance suffered. Finally, there was no accountability for the management since, first of all, its reward was not based on performance and, second, performance itself was influenced by some of the activities forced on the enterprise and not related to its core function.

Thus, by and large, the public sector has acted as a brake on private sector development. The choice of location, technology, employment, and pricing policies of the public sector had become, and continue to be, politicized so that efficient development was precluded. Far from generating resources, the public sector had become a monumental waste and liability for taxpayers. It is true that the industrialization strategy did generate a diversified industrial base and a capability for designing and fabricating industrial plants and machinery. But the strategy virtually ignored considerations of scale economies, vastly restricted domestic and import competition, constrained technological upgrading through licensing and purchase of foreign technologies, and encouraged capital-intensive production and discouraged employment generation that was further constrained by the high costs of hiring and firing imposed by our restrictive labour laws. In addition, there was very little flexibility to redeploy labour even *within* enterprises. The consequence was a high cost and globally uncompetitive industrial sector which was also out of tune with India's capital scarcity and labour abundance.

The reforms of 1991 abolished industrial licensing, except in a few industries for locational reasons or for environmental considerations, and import licensing, except in the case of most consumer goods. Restrictions under the Monopolies and Restrictive Trade Practices Act were eased. Entry requirements (including limits on equity participation) for foreign direct investment were relaxed. Private (domestic and foreign) investment were allowed into sectors such as power which had been reserved for public sector investment only. Disinvestment of equity in the public sector was also initiated. The reforms, by focusing primarily on the private sector and not addressing the problems of PSEs, have exacerbated them: while the PSEs can no longer expect their deficits to be financed through the budget, the ease of entry of private units in sectors that were public sector monopolies before reforms has worsened their deficits. Also, paradoxically even though industrial licensing has been abolished for most industries, PSEs still need ministerial and other bureaucratic clearances for their commercial decisions.

In commenting on the unfinished tasks of industrial reforms, I will focus my remarks on two broad areas. The first is *Industrial Sickness and Privatization* and the second is the *Small Scale Sector Reservation Policies*. Until there is a drastic reform of company and labour laws, particularly the Industrial Disputes Act, the problem of industrial sickness will neither go away nor be easily tackled. Indeed these laws, and the pressure from powerful trade unions on the government to take over failing private enterprises, preclude sensible approaches to deal with sickness. For example, in the United States, the so-called Chapter 11 of bankruptcy laws enables an orderly way of dealing with failing enterprises by providing them temporary protection from creditors during which period alternatives ranging from restructuring to closure are explored. India's Bureau for Industrial and Financial Restructuring (BIFR) has not performed this role to any significant extent. Between its inception in May 1987 and the end of November 1998, it received 3,441 references of which, 2,404 were registered and 452 were dismissed as non-maintainable under the Sick Industries Company Act of 1985. It recommended winding up 606 and rehabilitating another 637 and declared 214 as no longer sick. Out of the 225 PSEs that were referred, it registered 157, recommended winding up 29 and rehabilitating 50, and declared 6 to be no longer sick (Government of India 1999, p. 111). However most of the recommendations are yet to be implemented.

Let me turn to privatization of public sector enterprises. These could be divided into three categories: those producing (A) internationally tradeable goods and services, (B) non-tradeables, in particular those with the characteristics of natural monopolies, and (C) others.

The most important consideration in privatizing an enterprise is that once privatized it will perform more efficiently. For this to come about it is essential that a privatized enterprise will face adequate competition from other domestic and foreign enterprises.[4] After all, competition is the most effective means for efficiency improvement and for ensuring that the resources employed earn the maximum returns. In enterprises of category A, except for a few traded goods, such as fertilizers or wide-bodied passenger jet aircraft, where the global market structure is not competitive, competition is easily arranged. It is enough to allow unrestricted imports, initially with a moderate tariff, if necessary, to allow the newly privatized enterprise to adjust gradually to import competition. The tariff should then be

---

[4] In fact private firms had been insulated from import competition through import quotas and licensing and from internal competition through industrial licensing. This insulation led to their being inefficient as well, and also to the underestimation, if not outright disbelief, by the public of efficiency gains from privatization of PSE's.

progressively reduced over time with the schedule of reduction announced in advance. Since enterprises of category C are not natural monopolies, in principle there should be no insurmountable problems in ensuring competition.

Enterprises of Category B are the most difficult to privatize. This category includes the basic infrastructure services— electricity, water, telecommunication. Clearly, even if privatization merely creates a private monopoly some efficiency gains would still be achieved in the sense that a privately owned monopoly, unlike a publicly owned one, would have greater incentives for cost reduction. Because the distortion of monopoly pricing will remain, users of the enterprise's product will not reap much of the efficiency gains.

Consideration should be given to unbundling monopoly and potentially competitive elements in vertically integrated PSEs, for example, State Electricity Boards which generate, transmit, and distribute power. A number of issues arise in reforming these basic industries which until recently were state monopolies in most developing countries including India. Paul Joskow (1999) describes these issues at some length. He rightly points out the obvious fact that reforms, such as restructuring and/or privatization of public enterprises, are not ends in themselves but are means towards achieving other policy goals. The first step of course is to define with some clarity what these goals are. For example, in divestment through sale to private investors of equity in public enterprises, it is not clear how the percentage of equity in an enterprise that is to be sold to private investors was determined. It is true that not all public enterprises need be of the same significance to national priorities, and a one-size-fits-all approach need not be the most effective approach to reforming them. Yet there has to be some rationale for the choice of particular percentages, and none has been offered thus far. Furthermore, apart, even the government's commitment to disinvestment appears doubtful. For example, having established the Disinvestment Commission some time ago, the government has chosen to reduce its power by not letting it monitor the privatization process and eroded its credibility by failing to act on its recommendations: 50 public sector undertakings were referred to the Commission and it made recommendations regarding 41 of them. These recommendations are 'currently under various stages of implementation in the departments concerned' (Government of India 1998, p. 103). It is hard to avoid the conclusion that no action is likely to be taken anytime soon. Reducing the Commission's power and delaying actions on its recommendations send the most unfortunate signals about the disinvestment process to foreign and domestic investors who are the potential purchaser of divested equity.

Joskow suggests several goals for restructuring: the first one is to improve the ability to mobilize adequate resources to support investments to balance supply and demand efficiently. A second goal is to increase productivity by reducing operating costs and investing in more efficient plants and equipment. This goal is very relevant in our context. For example, our public sector fertilizer plants are of different capacities, were built at different times, and operate with different product mixes and technologies, particularly with respect to feed stocks for producing ammonia. The capacities range from the oldest, and perhaps the smallest, to the newer and much bigger plants. Until it was changed to use fuel oil as feed stock, the Nangal plant used very costly electricity for electrolysis of water to produce hydrogen that was combined with nitrogen and converted to ammonia. This plant was built in the 1950s, in part because of a colossal misperception then that electricity from the Bhakra dam would be forever in excess supply. Other plants have varied feedstocks such as naphtha, fuel oil, and coal. A large part of the problem of our fertilizer pricing, and the related issue of fertilizer subsidy, arose from the fact that the costs of fertilizers produced from these diverse plants varied substantially from each other and also from the prevailing world prices. The Fertilizer Pricing Committee, chaired by Hanumantha Rao (Department of Fertilizers 1998), has attempted to address some of these issues, but has unfortunately not recommended a fully market-based approach that will integrate domestic and world fertilizer markets, while recognizing that India, as a major importer, could potentially use its market power.

Joskow's third goal is to bring prices in line with costs (including non-priced environmental costs) to provide consumers with good price signals. Clearly this is an extremely important goal—needless to say that underpricing of electricity for agricultural use and the subsidization of nitrogenous fertilizers have resulted in an extremely distorted use of both water and fertilizers. Whether it is in the distribution of electricity or allocation of canal water, the government has either been unable, or worse, still unwilling (for political reasons) to tackle firmly with theft and violation of rules. Coupled with the underpricing, the inefficient and inequitable allocation of surface water from public irrigation systems has encouraged excessive use of ground water. Salinity and water logging and the loss of cultivable land as well as exploitation of aquifers beyond sustainable levels have been the outcomes of such excessive use.

The fourth and fifth goals involve respectively the need for the sector to generate enough surplus over costs to finance its own investment, and to ensure that those parts of the sector that remain in the public sphere charge prices that are compatible with the introduction of competition in areas to be privatized. Again the last objective is quite relevant in our context. If we were to privatize electricity generation as well as distribution to make them competitive, while retaining transmission as a public sector (or as a regulated private sector) monopoly, the fees charged for the use of the transmission grid will be of great significance to the efficiency and viability of competition in generation and transmission. The natural ebbs and flows of demand during the course of a day as well as across seasons, seasonal variation in supply from hydroelectric plants, and random shocks to supplies and demands require a structure of prices which adapts to these variations if overall efficiency of generation and distribution is to be achieved.

Apart from clarifying the goals to be achieved through privatization and restructuring, two other needed steps are to define a reform model that, as Joskow rightly says, has to go well beyond sloganeering and chanting the mantras of privatization, deregulation, and competition. The model has to define which segments of the industry will remain monopolies, albeit regulated ones, and which segments will be opened to competition. Even in the case of a regulated monopoly it is possible that future entry, and hence competition, are feasible and anticipated, in which case the regulation has to take this into account in its functioning. For the segments in which competition is to be introduced, the form of competition, mechanisms, and the sequencing and pace of their introduction have to be thought through. Finally, given that the eventual structure of the industry will include competitive and regulated monopolies as segments, the extent of horizontal integration in each level of the production chain and vertical integration between levels of the production chain ought to be clarified. For example, if electricity generation and distribution are to be privatized while transmission is a monopoly, should generating companies be allowed to have distribution subsidiaries? Should there be a national transmission monopoly or should there be many regional monopolies? Even more importantly should the transmission monopoly be allowed to own a generating or distribution subsidiary? In evaluating the recently introduced reforms of the electricity sector in Orissa, Rajasthan, and other states, it is important that these issues are thought through in some depth. The same issues arise in the telecommunication sector as well.

The legislation for enabling the setting up of a regulatory framework for electricity has been approved. The Security and Exchanges Board of India (SEBI) has been in operation for several years. A telecommunications regulatory authority of India (TRAI) has been established. However, issues regarding the organization of a regulatory agency such as its independence both from government and politics as well as from the industry it is to regulate, transparency of its procedures, its accountability, expertise, and credibility arise. Whether or not SEBI and TRAI made the correct decisions, the facts that the Finance Ministry on occasion chose to overrule the SEBI and that the Delhi High Court decided against a ruling of TRAI raise serious concerns about the autonomy of the two regulatory bodies. Be that as it may, the design of regulatory mechanisms for prices to be charged etc. are crucial. We seem to have uncritically accepted pan-territorial pricing of output, that is, uniform delivered prices throughout the country in many products, such as fertilizers. In the emerging structure this issue has to be revisited.

I have not so far touched on the managerial autonomy, particularly freedom to hire and fire, choose the wage and salary structure, etc. that any enterprise would need to function in a competitive environment. As far as the private sector is concerned, our labour laws, particularly the Industrial Disputes Act, severely constrain managerial autonomy. This is not to say that there are no other factors behind inefficiency in the private sector. Powerful trade unions and a supine, if not colluding, management have together ensured that even within firms labour is not efficiently allocated and that hierarchy and status, more than performance, influence decisions. In the case of public sector enterprises, despite memoranda of understanding, there has been little autonomy in practice for the management. It remains to be seen whether the autonomy promised for the so-called 'navaratnas' will in fact materialize.

Let me now turn to the small-scale sector reservation policy. This is partly a Gandhian legacy of protecting and promoting traditional handicrafts and 'cottage' or household production which should be distinguished from more modern and more organized small-scale sectors. It was in part also motivated by the desire to promote employment through labour-intensive manufactures. This policy has largely failed, although employment in the 'organized' small-scale sector grew faster than in large-scale manufacturing. A major victim of this unfortunate policy has been our cotton textile industry. Hobbled by the reservation to the handloom sector of a sizeable part of its market and by the restrictive policies relating to technology imports and import substitution regarding machinery, the textile industry was strangulated. In large part these policies contributed to the sickness in the industry. The reservation, rather than encouraging handlooms, gave rise to the powerloom sector. Paradoxically, the reservation policy penalized efficiency by taxing success: a small-sector firm which thrived under the reservation umbrella could not grow too much without losing the privilege of the benefits conferred on the small-scale sector.

The problems with reservation, particularly in the context of liberalization, are severe. A committee headed by Mr. Abid Hussain, which reported in 1997, concluded that the '. . . case for reservation is fundamentally flawed and self-contradictory . . . the policy crippled the growth of several industrial sectors, restricted exports and has done little for the promotion of small-scale industries' (p. 130, as quoted in World Bank 1998a, p. 27). As the latest World Bank (1998a) report points out, only *domestic large* firms are prevented from entering sectors reserved for small-scale production. *Foreign large* firms can now compete with domestic small-scale firms. In fact, according to the Hussain Committee Report, out of the 1,045 tariff lines that corresponded to products reserved for small-scale production, as many as 563 or 54 per cent are now under a free-trade regime! Fortunately, there is redundancy in reservation. There is *no* small-scale production of roughly a fifth of the reserved items. Because of its possible crippling effects on growth, firms try and often succeed in evading the reservation policy—there is some evidence that large firms have entered the powerloom and other consumer goods reserved for the small-scale sector, either directly or by other means.

Many of the reserved products are major export items, including garments accounting for a third or more of our exports. In contrast, large-scale manufacturers of non-reserved products have not shown great enthusiasm for exporting—the returns from sales to protected domestic markets were much higher for them. With the phase-out of the Multifibre Arrangement in 2005, unless our garment sector can compete effectively with other efficient producers in the world, our share in world markets will go down. On the other hand, if reservation is lifted, and constraints on the capacity expansion of successful small enterprises removed, large firms, domestic and foreign, would enter and ensure that not only do we not lose our market share but also increase it. The World Bank (1998a) Report also points out that some Indian joint ventures abroad (for example in Nepal) are a response to the domestic reservation policy—by moving abroad where there are no reservations and producing there for exports to India, Indian large firms in effect circumvent the reservation policy. Even if they do not move production abroad in response to reservation, Indian large firms would be tempted to fragment production in several small firms rather than produce in one large firm. These are avoidable costs imposed on large firms and the benefits, if any, in terms of employment generated in the small-scale sector do not seem to outweigh the costs.

I should also mention the reform of our labour and bankruptcy laws without which privatization and rehabilitation of sick enterprises cannot go very far. By making hiring and firing costly, labour laws have raised the cost of labour relative to capital—it should cause no surprise that while employment in organized manufacturing enterprises in the private sector hardly grew in the 1980s, output grew in part with steady investment, thus making production excessively capital-intensive. As Professor Mahalanobis (1969) pointed out long ago, certain welfare measures tend to be implemented in India ahead of economic growth, for example, in labour laws which are probably the most highly protective of labour interests in the narrowest sense, in the whole world. There is practically no link between output and remuneration; hiring and firing are highly restricted. It is extremely difficult to maintain an economic level of productivity or improve productivity . . . the present form of protection of organized labour, which constitutes, including their families, about five or six percent of the whole population, would operate as an obstacle to growth and would also increase inequalities. [Mahalanobis 1969, p. 442]

It is still the case that the employees of the public sector and organized manufacture are a labour aristocracy which is a small proportion of the labour force. This aristocracy enjoys relatively high wages, security of employment, pension and health benefits, housing allowance, paid vacation and leave travel concessions, and other perquisites none of which is available to the overwhelming majority of the labour force. It is nothing short of scandalous that our political leaders from the left to the right caved in to the demands of this aristocracy by being even more generous than the Fifth Pay Commission in setting their salaries while completely ignoring the other recommendations of the Commission regarding the growth of the bureaucracy.[5] Mahalanobis was surely right in suggesting that

it would seem better to try to attain the highest possible efficiency of labour and increasing productivity, and use the additional value obtained in this way to create more employment rather than lower the industrial efficiency by slack or restrictive practices through overstaffing. [Mahalanobis 1961, p. 157]

To the best of my knowledge, the National Renewal Fund, established in 1991 to ease the adjustment problems of labour laid off from enterprises to be restructured, has not been very

---

[5] It has been suggested that it is unfair to focus exclusively on the labour aristocracy without taking note at the same time of the rapid increases in the remuneration of the managerial cadre in private business since the reforms, and their consequent spill over effects on salaries for the senior bureaucracy. But to the extent that market forces determine managerial compensation on the one hand, and on the other, pay and perquisites of the labour aristocracy are sustained by restriction of labour laws, there is a difference between the rewards to managers and workers.

successful. In this connection, it is worth seriously considering the proposal of Mahalanobis for setting up a Labour Reserve (LR)

to absorb such industrial workers as may be considered surplus and be 'laid off' by existing industrial enterprises at their discretion, and also to serve as a pool for other enterprises to draw upon, again, at their own discretion. The Labour Reserve Service (LR) would then act as a buffer against unemployment and would serve as a (perhaps socially more useful and psychologically more preferable) form of or substitute for unemployment insurance. . . . The LR would provide training of various kinds and would continually try to use the men for productive purposes. Workers in the LR would have an incentive to find better jobs at the earliest opportunity. [ibid., pp. 157–8]

2

Agriculture[1]

Agriculture is the most important sector of the Indian economy from the perspective of poverty alleviation and the related goal of employment generation. Nearly two-thirds of our labour force depends on agriculture for gainful employment. Casual agricultural labourers, tenants and share-croppers, and marginal and small farmers together account for a large share of the rural poor. Yet it is the one sector which has been largely left out of the process of economic liberalization and reforms initiated in July 1991. In a superficial sense, because the plethora of government controls on investment, output, imports, technology, location choice, that affected the industrial sector had no counterparts in the agricultural sector, it might seem that there was less scope for the reform process to encompass agriculture. However, as I will argue, there were many government interventions in agriculture, including those that kept Indian agriculture insulated from world markets. There is no question that these have to be reformed.

Let me recall some salient facts about Indian agriculture. The trend rate of growth of agricultural output of the country as a whole has remained constant since the 1950s at about 2.5 per cent to 3 per cent per annum. However, the constancy of aggregate growth masks several significant changes. First, the contributions of area expansion and yield growth to the growth of output have changed significantly during the last five decades. Between 1950–1 and 1970–1, before the green revolution technology based on high yielding varieties of cereals, introduced in the

---

[1] In preparing this chapter I have benefited and drawn from my conversations with economists at the World Bank on their forthcoming report on India's rural development.

late sixties, made much headway, area under all crops grew by 30 per cent and the index of yield per unit area grew by 43 per cent. But between 1970–1 and 1996–7 area growth shrunk to just 11 per cent, while yield growth shot up to 61 per cent, reflecting primarily the effects of the green revolution (Government of India 1998, Tables 1.9, 1.10 and 1.11, pp. S-13–S-15). Second, the contribution of different regions and crops to the aggregate growth have changed as well. For example, the eastern states of Assam, Bihar, Orissa, and West Bengal taken together, and West Bengal in particular, have performed dramatically better in the 1980s and 1990s than they did in the previous three decades. Among crops, production of oilseeds doubled in the decade between the triennia of 1984–7 and 1994–7. Third, the relative contribution of *Kharif* crops, particularly cereals, to annual output has declined over the years. In 1996–7, output of *Kharif* cereals was 99 million tonnes as compared to the *Rabi* output of 86 million tonnes (ibid., Table 1.12, p. S-16). In 1970–1, the *Kharif* output at 65 million tonnes was more than twice the *Rabi* output of 32 million tonnes. Fourth, near self-sufficiency, albeit at relatively low levels of consumption, has been attained with respect to foodgrains and oilseeds. Needless to say, many of these changes are in response to the policies pursued. It is also the case that some of these trends have been costly.

Let me note a disquieting recent development. According to the World Bank, in agriculture, growth in total factor productivity (TFP), which is a comprehensive measure of technical progress, has turned to a *negative* 0.59 per cent per year in the first half of the 1990s, as compared to a healthy (and *positive*) 1.39 per cent annual average in the 1970s, which accelerated to 1.99 per cent in the 1980s.[2] Five states, Assam, Gujarat, Haryana, Madhya Pradesh, and Rajasthan, recorded larger declines in TFP in the first half of the 1990s compared to the 1980s. In Maharashtra and Tamil Nadu, TFP registered a decline as opposed to growth, and in Andhra Pradesh and West Bengal there was a slower, but positive, growth in the latter period. Only in the states of Bihar, Orissa, Karnataka, and Kerala was there acceleration in TFP growth. Clearly productivity growth is the source for increases in

---

[2] Conceptual and measurement problems are significant in measuring TFP. The estimates quoted have to be used with these problems in mind.

factor returns, including returns to labour. Unsurprisingly, the slowdown in productivity growth seems to have had an impact on the average rate of growth of real wages in rural areas—it declined from a healthy 3.56 per cent per annum in the 1980s to a measly 0.77 per cent during 1990–3 which included a poor agricultural-cum-macroeconomic crisis year of 1991–2. However except in 1994–5 it has increased in every year until 1997–8 (Government of India 1999, p. 145).

Let me now turn to the policies affecting the agricultural sector and their reform. Almost all governments in the world intervene in markets for agricultural commodities. In India, with overlapping jurisdiction over the agricultural sector between the centre and the states, there have been a large number of policy interventions. There is no evidence that these interventions have been coordinated to achieve a well-defined set of policy objectives. Quite the contrary—it would not be difficult to cite examples of mutually inconsistent policies being pursued. Also, policies relating to foreign trade, exchange rates, and industry have had not only large but also offsetting effects on agriculture. Again, World Bank (1996, Table 4.1) estimates suggest that during 1970–85, agricultural policies disprotected agriculture as a whole by 4.0 per cent, which turned to positive protection at the rate of 7 per cent during 1985–91. Yet disprotection from economy-wide policies remained constant at around 25 per cent, so that disprotection of agriculture fell from about 30 per cent in the first period to 18 per cent in the second. Post-1991 reforms have vastly reduced the disprotection from economy-wide policies—to only 3 per cent during 1994–5. However, agricultural policies are disprotected to a larger extent at 7 per cent so that total disprotection is still 10 per cent.

It is useful to organize the discussion of the possible reforms of agricultural sector policies into those relating to foreign trade, inputs such as fertilizer, water and fuel, infrastructure such as transportation and communication, outputs, processing, distribution, and marketing. Although it is no longer politically correct to talk about land and tenancy reforms, let me note that although 'Operation Barga' of West Bengal has successfully registered share-croppers, thereby providing security of the terms of tenure, it is unlikely that other states will follow. There is also some controversy on the contribution of Operation Barga to the apparent acceleration of agricultural growth in West Bengal in the 1980s.

Although overall protection and disprotection through agricultural trade policies has been relatively small, there have been substantial variations in the rates of protection across commodities. Non-tariff barriers in terms of quantitative restrictions and monopolization, or to use the Indian term, canalization, of trade by state enterprises have been, and continue to be, far more significant than tariffs. According to the World Bank (1998a, Annex Table 8), prior to 1991, almost all of the tradeable agricultural commodities were protected by non-tariff barriers. Exports of most agricultural goods, except traditional exports— tea, coffee, spices, and jute were subject to quantitative restrictions. In the 1950s and 1960s, there were export taxes on traditional exports. Although there was significant trade liberalization between 1991 and 1995, there have been reversals since. By 1997–8, coverage of agricultural imports through non-tariff barriers has come down from near 100 per cent to only 80 per cent. There are barriers on imports of rice and wheat as well as other commodities, accounting for more than three quarters of agricultural products. Quantitative restrictions apply with respect to exports of most commodities, except basmati rice and durum wheat.

It is clear that Indian agriculture is very far from being integrated with world markets. Such integration clearly should be of the highest priority, while paying due attention to the fact that in some commodities, such as rice, world prices would be significantly affected if India were to trade large amounts. The potential for agricultural exports, of traditional as well as non-traditional products such as cut flowers and fresh fruits, is vast. But without an adequate infrastructure, particularly for exports of perishables and for pre-shipment inspection and quality grading, this potential will not be realized. I should also mention that India will not be viewed as a reliable exporter, and hence will not realize its export potential, if the political fall out feared from increases in the prices of sensitive commodities leads to periodic bans on their exports. There is of course the infamous example of onions, the exports of which were banned once in Mrs. Gandhi's days and several times since. The other example is exports of raw cotton, which are periodically restricted in order to contain any increase in the price of cotton that domestic textile mills have to pay. Clearly, the possibility that an export ban could be imposed on the whims of politicians is not exactly conducive to the long-term development of export markets. Since domestic prices of wheat and rice are lower than their border prices, and those of oilseeds and sugar higher, full integration with world markets will result in increases in the domestic prices of the former and decreases in those of the latter two commodities. However, with integration phased in gradually, and with a well targeted safety net in place for the poor, the adverse effects of integration on the poor, if any, could be mitigated.

In the absence of trade barriers and domestic interventions, with stable exchange rates, domestic prices will follow the same trend as world prices.[3] Our exchange rate has not remained stable and domestic interventions have been significant, though varying across commodities. For example, between 1990–1 and 1994–5 real world prices of oilseeds increased by 12 per cent and the rupee depreciated by 26 per cent in real terms. But because domestic interventions reduced prices received by producers by 62 per cent, the domestic real price received by oil seed producers declined by 22 per cent (World Bank 1996, Table 4.2). Whether or not it is a desirable policy to allow fluctuations in world prices to pass through without interference into the domestic economy is a separate and complex issue. But even if stabilization of prices is desirable, it would seem that integration with world markets, rather than insulation from them, would indeed be more stabilizing in many commodities.

Even within India, the markets for agricultural commodities are not integrated. Restrictions on the movement of commodities across states, and even within states, are often imposed to serve narrow parochial interests of groups within individual states at the

---

[3] Note that world trade in agricultural commodities is distorted by interventions in major exporting countries such as the European Union and the United States. The Uruguay Round Agreement did not eliminate these distortions. The scheduled review of the agricultural agreement in year 2000 is likely to reduce them. However the impact on world prices of complete elimination of distortions is likely to be modest if the simulations from global general equilibrium models (for example, Parikh *et al.* 1988) are to be believed.

expense of the population of the rest of the country. For example, Gujarat, a major groundnut oil producer, has imposed restrictions on the export of its production in times of below normal production. But Gujarat is by no means unique in imposing such restrictions. In Maharashtra there is a state operated cotton procurement monopoly that restricts farmers' sales of cotton at higher prices in neighbouring states.

Turning now to the input side, public spending on agriculture as a proportion of agricultural GDP in India has been much higher than in some Asian countries, such as Indonesia, Malaysia, and Thailand, while Indian agricultural growth has been slower (World Bank 1996, Table 4.3). The World Bank (1996) suggests two broad reasons for this: the first is that the composition of public spending across categories, regions, or states is not geared towards a more rapid, broad-based, and poverty alleviating agricultural growth. Second, not only is the public spending very much skewed towards subsidies, and against growth-enhancing investment and expenditures on operation and maintenance of existing stock of capital, but also such skewing contributes to the poor quality and reliability of delivery of inputs such as power and water. Clearly the scale as well as composition of public spending on agriculture have to be rethought and restructured.

Let me turn to reforms relating to input supplies starting with irrigation. There can be no doubt, that our existing system is extremely inefficient and iniquitous. We have reached the stage where the possibilities of further expansion of surface irrigation through large storage systems are almost exhausted, except perhaps through joint development of hydroelectric power with Nepal and Bangladesh and even this is likely to draw objections from environmentalists. As such, development of ground water resources, as well as improvement in the efficiency of use of the existing system, are extremely important. Also, the rates of return to investments in operations improvement and modernization of existing systems are much higher than from investments in new major and minor irrigation projects. The experience from the investment in the improvement of the Bhadra scheme in Karnataka amply confirms this. Not only did irrigated area and paddy area increase substantially, but water use per hectare of crop area came down by over 20 per cent due to efficiency gains. But such efficiency and equity gains can be achieved only with major revamping of state irrigation departments and even more importantly with the involvement of farmers in the operation of the system. Again this is not something new—several ideas, including the formation of water users' associations, have been proposed. Some of these have been implemented in Pakistan and Bangladesh and in Andhra Pradesh as well. Of course, any reform of the irrigation system has to ensure that users face the true cost of delivery so that the cost of operating and maintaining the system, including a capital charge for generating surpluses for further investment, is recovered. The Committee on Irrigation Pricing under the chairmanship of Dr A. Vaidynathan has extensively discussed the issues of pricing and organizational-cum-managerial reforms. But such reforms are most unlikely in our political climate.

Turning now to the subsidized provision of electricity to farmers, several points are worth making. First of all, such subsidization naturally led to the greater use of ground water than would have been the case without the subsidy. Given that in India, rights to ground water rest with the owner of the land, there is nothing to prevent uncoordinated pumping from the same aquifer by several farmers who own land over it with the consequence that more water is pumped out than can be sustained. In turn, water tables decline, pumping costs increase, and in coastal areas salt water intrusion into aquifers takes place. In other areas, water logging has been the result of poor drainage. Recovering land that has become saline or water-logged is costly.

Second, subsidizing an input, be it electricity, diesel, or fertilizer, is appropriate only if the intention is to increase the use of that input beyond what would be the case without the subsidy. If the intention is in fact to raise output, an output subsidy, rather than an input subsidy, is the better instrument. If the intention is distributional, that is, if the subsidy is meant to ensure that poor farmers are enabled to use the input to a greater extent than they would have otherwise done, the subsidy has to be one that is effectively targeted so that only poor farmers and not others have access to it. None of our input subsidies are targeted; yet, the name of the small and marginal farmers is invariably invoked by the politicians in justifying such subsidies. Again, if poverty alleviation, rather than enabling poor farmers to use the input to a greater extent, is the objective, an input subsidy is not the appropriate instrument; instead, a direct income support of the poor is more suitable.

Third, since the electricity boards bear the cost of subsidy by charging a low price or even nothing as in Tamil Nadu and Punjab for electricity, the quality and reliability of supply is affected. Thus farmers, although paying a low or even zero tariff, receive power that is often erratic, fluctuates in voltage, and is supplied at odd hours. A World Bank study reports that because of the poor quality and unreliability of supplies, the effective cost of power for the farmer ranges between Rs. 0.90 and Rs. 3.53 per kwh in contrast to the proposed subsidized price of Rs. 0.50 per kwh. Clearly this suggests that farmers might be willing to pay a higher price for power if its supply is reliable, timely, and of high quality (for example without fluctuations in voltage). In addition to electricity supplied free there is also theft of power that is subsumed under transmission and distribution losses. Some estimates suggest that as much as a fourth of electricity generated is either stolen or supplied free. These loses to the public exchequer are large and not justified by any social rationale.

Fertilizer pricing and subsidy policies have a long history, in part stemming from the import-substituting industrialization strategy pursued by the country for over four decades. Indeed, as I mentioned in my first lecture, the subsidy in large part reflects the high cost of our fertilizer industry which consists of plants of various vintages, less than efficient sizes, and different technologies using a plethora of feedstocks. Some plants are owned by the government and others by cooperatives and the private sector. The fertilizer pricing committees (Department of Fertilizers 1998) pointed out that the present retention pricing scheme for producers is a prescription for inefficiency. I do not wish to discuss the recommendations of the committee except to reiterate that many of the issues, such as lack of clarity about the objectives of subsidization, the instruments used to subsidize, etc., that I raised in discussing electricity subsidies apply in the case of fertilizer subsidies.

Let me conclude by touching very lightly upon four issues. First, there is no question that there is a continuing role for agricultural research and extension. In the contemporary global context there is a potential for involving the private sector (domestic and foreign) in bringing better crop varieties, seeds, and techniques to our agriculture.[4] Also, modern information and communication technologies offer innovative ways of extending new ideas and techniques to the farmer. These have to be explored. Second, agriculture has largely remained out of the direct tax base since land revenue has virtually gone out of existence. As greater, and rapidly growing, income earning opportunities in agriculture arise, in part due to enabling public policies, it is only fair that agricultural incomes are brought into the tax base. A number of ways of doing so, while paying due regard to the inherent riskiness of agriculture, are well known and one or more of them should be introduced as soon as possible. Third, the laudable attempt since 1985 to provide insurance to farmers against risks of crop failures has not been very successful. For example, claims paid out at Rs. 15.23 billion far exceed Rs. 2.69 billion of premiums collected (Government of India 1998, p. 119). Here again alternatives such as rainfall-based or soil-moisture based insurance schemes have been proposed. Their feasibility and cost-effectiveness in our context have to be examined. However a general point needs to be made about risks: in India all industrialists, farmers, and organized workers expect the state to fully absorb any downside risks (be they from natural calamities or from policy changes) and the state has fulfilled their expectations at high cost. In a reformed environment in which upside potential has been raised, it is essential that some of the downside risks are borne by the beneficiaries themselves rather than by the state. Finally, the ongoing reforms of the agricultural credit have to be extended, deepened, and accelerated. The recovery of agricultural advances by commercial banks is still (as of 1996) only 61 per cent of the amounts due (ibid., Table 8.16).

---

[4] There are some legitimate concerns that protections offered to patents and other intellectual property rights under the TRIPS component of the Uruguay Round agreement, to which India is a signatory, could hurt our interests. It is important that in the scheduled review of the TRIPS agreement in year 2000 we push for a world-wide system for the recognition and rewarding of the informal innovation of our traditional communities to conservation of biodiversity and to knowledge of traditional plant-based medicines and cures.

3

Poverty Alleviation[1]

Eradication of poverty has long been the overarching objective of Indian economic development. Of course, the early classic study on Indian poverty is Dadabhai Naoroji's (1901), *Poverty and Un-British Rule in India*. The National Planning Committee chaired by Pandit Nehru stated in 1948 that the objective of planning, 'was to insure an adequate standard of living for the masses; in other words, to get rid of the appalling poverty of the people . . . the irreducible, in terms of money, had been estimated by economists at figures varying from Rs. 15 to Rs. 25 per capita per month' (Nehru 1946, pp. 402–3). This figure quoted by Panditji was at prices prevailing prior to the Second World War. As such the committee's poverty line was considerably more generous than the consumption expenditure of Rs. 20 per capita at 1960–1 prices that would be set as the rural poverty line by the Planning Commission in 1960.

All the pre-independence plans for Indian development, including those of the National Planning Committee, Sir M. Visveswaraya, the Indian Federation of Labour, and a group of Bombay businessmen, identified poverty as the central problem of the Indian economy. The authors of the Bombay Plan also proposed a poverty line at about Rs. 75 per capita income per year at pre-war prices, a much more modest poverty line than that proposed by Panditji's committee.

This history enables me to make two points: the first is the obvious failures to achieve our modest poverty reduction targets

[1] I have drawn from my conversations with Martin Ravallion at the World Bank on the ongoing research on poverty alleviation in India at the Bank, in particular its latest (World Bank 1998b) poverty assessment.

and to attain the needed growth. Thus even after nearly fifty years of planning since independence, more than a third of our population (36 per cent in 1993–4, according to World Bank 1998b, p. 1) still has a monthly consumption below our extremely modest poverty line. In terms of absolute number, there were 320 million poor in 1993–4 or roughly double the number of 164 million in 1950. Second, contrary to the assertion by western economists and agencies such as the United Nations Development Programme (UNDP) that developing countries were fixated on income growth and neglected poverty alleviation and human development, *in India the objective has never been growth per se but only growth as an instrument for poverty alleviation.*

The remarkable paper, prepared in 1962 at the Perspective Planning Division of the Planning Commission under the leadership of the late Pitambar Pant (Srinivasan and Bardhan 1974, pp. 2–38), defined the poverty line at a consumption expenditure of Rs. 20 per capita at 1960–1 prices, and envisaged eradicating poverty in fifteen years from 1960–1. The paper explicitly argued for rapid growth as *the* instrument for poverty alleviation, while at the same time recognizing the need for redistributive transfers to those poor who, for various reasons, were either unconnected or weakly connected with the income generation processes in the economy. The growth target of national income set in this paper was 7 per cent per year for the decade 1966–76. Earlier, Sir M. Visveswaraya had proposed the doubling of national income in ten years, which implied a 7 per cent annual rate of growth. Panditji's committee wished to at least double, if not triple, national income in ten years. The Bombay Plan aimed to double per capita income in fifteen years, which would have meant an annual growth rate of about 6 per cent in national income given the then rate of growth of the population of about 1 per cent a year. In the post-independence era, except for the modest first five year plan, every other five year plan envisaged more than 5 per cent growth in national income per year. But none of these goals were reached. The average rate of growth achieved in the forty seven years since we began planning in 1950 is about 4 per cent. For the three decades until the beginning of the sixth plan in 1980–1, the average rate of growth was even less at 3.5 per cent per annum, the infamous Hindu rate of growth.

It is this massive failure to achieve rapid growth that is the root cause of our failure to eliminate poverty. The World Bank (1997, Table 2.1) reports that the poverty head count ratio goes down by almost 1 per cent for every 1 per cent increase in net domestic product (NDP) per capita. Had per capita NDP grown by 5 per cent per year since 1950–1, per capita NDP in 1997–8 would have been ten times that for 1950–1. Other things remaining the same, given a unitary elasticity, the head count poverty ratio now would have been about 4.5 per cent in 1997–8, one-tenth its 1950–1 value of around 45 per cent (World Bank 1998b, p. 1). Alternatively, if poverty is to be halved in ten years from its 1993–4 value of 36 per cent, per capita income has to double in ten years or grow by 7.1 per cent a year. The analysis of Demery and Walton (1998) using cross-country regressions, rather than time series analysis of Indian data, and an international poverty line consumption of $2 a day suggest that halving India's poverty would require a 5 per cent growth rate per capita per year between 1990 and 2015. We need not take these calculations literally to argue the vital importance of considerably accelerating our rate of growth if we wish to make a serious dent on the appalling poverty of our people. The quality or character of growth, and not simply its rate, is also crucial for poverty alleviation: growth has to enhance the prospects of the poor. Before discussing policies that will accelerate growth and ensure that it encompasses the poor, let me just say here that in East Asia, until the recent crisis, growth was both rapid and poverty reducing.

Apart from the tried and tested policy of rapid and shared growth, other poverty alleviation policies include transfers of various kinds and policies that augment the earned income of poor households. The two main transfer programmes in India are the Public Distribution System (PDS) and the provision of Integrated Child Development Services (ICDS). Other transfers include pensions to widows and the elderly. There are several income-augmenting programmes: the Integrated Rural Development Programme (IRDP), Development of Women and Children in Rural Areas (DWCRA), Training of Youth and Self-employment Programmes (TRYSEMS), and two public works programmes for employment generation, namely Jawahar Rozgar Yojana (JRY) and the Employment Assurance Scheme (EAS).

Area based programmes include Drought Prone Areas Programme (DPAP) and Watershed Programmes. Some of these programmes overlap with each other.

The first important point to note is that in 1997–8 spending by the central government on all major poverty alleviation and basic needs programmes, narrowly defined, taken together accounted for 8.9 per cent of the central plan budgetary expenditure (World Bank 1998b, Table 4.1) or a modest 1.45 per cent of the gross domestic product (GDP).[2] The situation is unlikely to change much in the five years following from 1997–8. In addition, more than a third of this expenditure is accounted for by the untargeted food subsidy of the PDS. Thus it would be a distortion to say that a lot has been spent on anti-poverty programmes—in the same year, 1997–8, the central government alone spent nearly 0.84 per cent of the GDP on explicit subsidies other than food, including the subsidy on fertilizers (World Bank 1998a, Table A4.11). Implicit subsidies of the centre, and the explicit and implicit subsidies of state governments, have to be added to this figure.

The further important point is that even the meagre expenditures on anti-poverty programmes were largely misspent and cost-ineffective. It is as if one were pouring a little water into a leaky bucket; obviously not much would remain in the bucket. The study of Radhakrishna and Subbarao (1997) is very revealing. They find that in 1986–7, the PDS and other consumer subsidy programmes accounted for less than 2.7 per cent of the per capita expenditure of the poor in rural areas and 3.2 per cent in the urban areas. The impact on poverty and the nutritional status of the population was minimal. The PDS had at most brought down the poverty ratio to 38 per cent from 40 per cent that year, a small reduction indeed. What is even more disturbing, the abolition of the PDS would have had a negligible impact in the rural areas where more than three-fourths of the poor live. The cost of the transfer through the PDS and other subsidies was

[2] If we define poverty alleviation programmes broadly enough to include outlays on rural and area development and social welfare under state plans, the expenditures would naturally be much larger. I do not think such a broad definition is warranted—it almost amounts to including *any* development expenditure as poverty alleviating.

very high. The World Bank (1998b, Table 4.2, p. 39) reports that the participation of the poorest quintile in the population in the PDS as compared to the average is lower at 92 per cent and the next two quintiles participate at a slightly higher rate than the average. Even the marginal odds of participation, that is the gain for each quintile following a rupee increase in aggregate spending on the PDS, is only 1.06 for the poorest quintile as compared to 0.81 for the richest quintile (ibid., Table 4.3, p. 41). Thus the PDS subsidies are not particularly pro-poor in their incidence. The central government alone spent more than 4.25 rupees to transfer one rupee to the poor. Combining central and state government expenditures, in Andhra Pradesh it took 6.35 rupees to transfer one rupee to the poor. The most cost-effective scheme was the ICDS which cost 1.80 rupees to transfer one rupee to the poor.

The employment generation programmes, which are in principle self-targeting, have the potential to be most cost effective. For example, according to the figures quoted by Radhakrishna and Subbarao (1997), in Bangladesh the leakage to the non-poor under their analogue of our PDS was as high as 70 per cent, while in the employment oriented programmes it ranged between 0 and 36 per cent. The cost per taka of transfer was as high as 6.55 in the former and between 1.32 and 1.49 in the latter. Unfortunately, our employment programmes are far from realizing their potential. In 1993–4, JRY programmes did generate nearly 1 billion person days of employment, a third of the estimated underemployment in the country. Yet during 1992, a JRY worker got on average about four days of employment in a month and the worker's family in all got a little over five days of employment. However, the average wage of the JRY worker was higher than the prevailing wage, thereby reducing its potential for self-targeting. In other words, a JRY worker was not necessarily poor. Taking this mistargeting into account, it cost about 4.35 rupees to transfer one rupee to the poor through the JRY.[3] Still, compared to the PDS, the incidence of expenditure on public works (PW) and integrated rural development (IRD) programmes are much more pro-poor. The marginal odds of

---

[3] The JRY is not even well targeted regionally in the sense the states are not allocated funds in proportion to their poverty levels.

participation of the poorest (respectively richest) quintile in the PW and IRD programmes respectively were 1.16 (respectively 0.50) and 1.11 (respectively 0.39), as per World Bank (1998b, Table 4.3, p. 45).

The difficulty of targeting and its politicization are clearly seen in Madhya Pradesh (MP). When bureaucrats did the targeting in the IRDP, they missed quite a few poor and included many non-poor, but there was an upper limit on mistargeting, namely the known proportion of poor in the area. But once the targeting was transferred to the Panchayats, the list of beneficiaries became grossly inflated—for example, in the Sagar district of MP *every* household was deemed poor enough to be a beneficiary of the IRDP! In some JRY programmes in Bihar, village pathways and roads had been constructed, but not by using workers from the villages themselves. In one district, wells had been repaired, and bridges built, but no respondent from the district reported being employed in these activities. In the same district it was reported by the respondents that the Pradhan in charge recorded a project had been completed in a scheduled tribe Basti while in fact it had been completed in his own upper-caste area. In another instance, the JRY programme was contracted out but the contractor did not pay the workers what was due to them.[4]

I hope I have said enough to convince you that our concern with poverty alleviation has mostly remained at the rhetorical level. The policies and public expenditures that have been explicitly poor-oriented or have been justified on their poverty alleviation impacts have been modest in scale and very ineffective and costly in their execution. What about those expenditures, particularly those on health and education that could potentially help the poor? Here again the situation is dismal, as I will argue in Chapter 5.

It is not surprising that, as compared to growth, redistributive policies contributed only modestly to the equally modest reduction in poverty alleviation over the last four decades. World Bank (1997, Table A.5) reports that of about 17 per cent

---

[4] In emphasizing poor targeting, I do not mean to ignore the potential for greater impact from current programmes through greater participation of the poor in their design and implementation, ensuring that outlays augment the stock of productive assets to a greater extent and locating projects in areas with greater concentration of the poor.

reduction in the poverty ratio between 1951–5 and 1993–4, as much as 15 per cent was accounted for by growth in real per capita consumption, with redistribution contributing only 2 per cent. Accelerating growth and making it more poor-oriented are the only efficacious long-term solutions to the problem of poverty.

Turning to the issue of making growth poor-oriented, it is useful to begin with the well known correlates of poverty in India. If one is poor in India, one is more likely to live in rural areas, more likely to be a member of the Scheduled Caste or Tribe or other socially discriminated groups, more likely to be malnourished, sick and in poor health, more likely to be illiterate or poorly educated and with low skills, more likely to live in certain states (such as the 'Bimaru' states of Bihar, Madhya Pradesh, Rajasthan, and Uttar Pradesh, and also Orissa) than in others, more likely to be a landless agricultural worker, wage earner or a marginal farmer, etc. Also the inequalities in education and health, mortality and morbidity, between males and females, particularly children, are higher among the poor than among the non-poor. What all these mean is that a pro-poor growth strategy will create rapidly expanding job opportunities in the rural areas in particular, on-farm and off-farm. It will emphasize the accumulation of human capital by the poor by addressing the inefficiencies and inequities in the health and education sector. I would also argue that an effective strategy will involve the private sector, particularly non-governmental organizations, in many activities where they can be more effective and will confine government involvement only to those areas where there is no more effective and efficient private alternative. While decentralization of government and devolution of both power and resources to local bodies are very desirable, I am not entirely certain whether the socially discriminated groups will fare any better with local Panchayats, rather than the state or central administration making decisions. Indeed, the World Bank (1998b, Table 2.6, p. 24) presents data that suggest that the service quality could drop by as much as 40 per cent if a service is funded at the village level rather than at the central or state level.

Reforms in other areas, such as completing trade liberalization by extending it to include agricultural and consumer goods, repealing or amending our labour and bankruptcy laws to allow managerial autonomy in employment decisions, strengthening the financial sector by tackling the overhang of non-performing loans of banks, and reducing the extent of directed credit and of politicization of the credit allocation process are important from the perspective of poverty alleviation as well. There are several reasons for this, the most important ones being that such reforms will accelerate income growth thereby alleviating poverty and will also result in more rapid employment generation through a reduction of costs of hiring. Trade liberalization, in particular, would increase the incentives for the manufacture and export of labour-intensive products in which we have a comparative advantage. Employment opportunities arising from such export growth will be poverty-alleviating. It is an unfortunate fact that we have been losing our share of world markets in these products to our competitors, particularly China (Srinivasan 1998, Table 9.3). For example, China gained substantially, while India barely managed to maintain its market share in exports of garments and textiles between 1979–81 and 1992–4. During the same period, India's share of exports of leather and leather manufactures fell substantially, while China's share increased dramatically.

I will conclude by endorsing, with all the emphasis that I can command, the conclusions emerging from the vast literature on poverty in India and policies for its alleviation, that are aptly summarized in the World Bank's *Report on Poverty* in India (1998b, p. 49):

Anti-poverty programs that either do not reach the poor or that bestow a disproportionate share of their benefits on the non-poor are programs in urgent need of reform. The majority of India's safety-net initiatives are misusing scarce financial resources that could be best invested to increase the poor's access to health and education services that have been shown to equip the poor to help themselves. Reform is not needed for its own sake but for the sake of India's poor and in the interests of having them both contribute to the growth process and benefit from it.

4

Fiscal Issues

Until the early 1980s India's macroeconomic policies were conservative. Current revenues of the central government exceeded current expenditures so that there was a surplus available to finance in part the deficit on capital account, a deficit that is normal for a developing country. In the early 1980s, fiscal prudence was abandoned, with the consequence that current revenue surpluses turned into deficits. This meant that the government had to borrow at home and abroad, not only to finance its investment as would normally be the case in a developing country, but also its current consumption.

Fiscal deficits, as published in government budget documents, have tended to understate the real imbalances. The reason was that the rates of interest at which the government appropriated a large share of the loanable resources of the banking system, through the statutory liquidity ratio (38.5 per cent maximum) and the cash reserve ratio (15 per cent maximum), were administratively set below what would have been market clearing levels. Also, at least in the early years, external borrowing was largely on concessional terms from multilateral lending institutions and from bilateral government to government external aid transactions. As the 1980s wore on, the government also resorted to borrowing from abroad on commercial terms, both from the capital market and non-resident Indians. In 1983–4, out of $22.8 billion of public and publicly guaranteed external debt, roughly 17 per cent was owed to private creditors. On the eve of the macroeconomic crisis in 1990–1, external debt had tripled to $69.3 billion, of which around 30 per cent was owed to private creditors (World Bank 1996, Table 3.1(a)). Thus debt to private creditors grew five-fold in seven years. The balance of the gross fiscal deficit, after taking into account the domestic and external borrowings, small savings, and provident funds, was monetized through the ad hoc sale of treasury bills to the Reserve Bank. For example, in 1988–9 and 1989–90, before the crisis year of 1991, the gross fiscal deficits of the centre and states together was rupees 35,668 and 45,196 crores respectively, and nearly 17 to 25 per cent of these sums, namely 6,244 crores and 10,911 crores respectively, were financed by the issue of *ad hoc* treasury bills (World Bank 1998a, Table A4.4).

Clearly the reckless fiscal expansionism of the 1980s was unsustainable. But accompanied by some liberalization in the form of delicensing of some industries and permitting flexible use of capacity in others through changes in product-mix within the licensed capacity under so-called 'broad banding' and relaxation of some import restrictions, generate growth. Indeed there was a mini-industrial boom during 1985–8. The average annual rate of growth of real gross domestic product (GDP) in the sixth and seventh plans which covered the 1980s was 5.5 per cent or 5.8 per cent respectively, much higher than the Hindu rate of growth of 3.5 per cent of the earlier three decades. As I mentioned in Chapter 3, the 1980s covered the major part of the period of a steep reduction in the proportion of poor in our population— from 51.3 per cent in 1977–8 to 38.9 per cent in 1987–8. Needless to say, the reduction in poverty achieved during a period of unsustainable debt-led growth could not have lasted. When the macroeconomic crisis hit in 1990–1, the gross fiscal deficit had grown to about 10 per cent of GDP at market prices. If one includes the losses of the non-financial public sector enterprises, the consolidated public sector deficit stood at around 12.3 per cent of the GDP in 1990–1. More than a third of this deficit, nearly 4.8 per cent of the GDP, was for interest payments on domestic and external debt. An analysis by Willem Buiter and Urjit Patel (1992) showed that unless corrective steps were taken, India faced fiscal insolvency.

It is no surprise therefore that one of the major objectives of Dr Manmohan Singh's reforms was to reduce the central government's fiscal deficit from 8.3 per cent of the GDP in 1990–1 to around 4 per cent or lower in three years or so. In fact, he did achieve a significant reduction to 5.9 per cent in 1991–2, his first full year as Finance Minister, and further to 5.7 per cent in

1992–3. But then it ballooned to 7.4 per cent in 1993–4. The deficit is estimated at 6.1 per cent in 1997–8 and is budgeted to come down to 5.8 per cent in 1998–9 (World Bank 1998a, Figure 1 and Annex Table 2). The budget for 1999–2000 projects a further reduction to a little over 4 per cent of the GDP. But with the unexpected conflict in Kargil and the associated increase in defence spending, it is unlikely that the projection for 1999–2000 will be realized. What is more, the consolidated non-financial public sector deficit, which incudes the deficits of central, state, and non-financial public sector undertakings, has remained at around 9.1 per cent of GDP or more since 1992–3 (World Bank 1998a, Annex Table 2).[1]

Studies of the experience of a cross section of countries suggest that large public sector deficits reduce growth by crowding out productive private investment. Attempts to reduce the mone-tization of deficit through domestic borrowing raise interest rates and reduce the profitability of investment. Some studies (World Bank 1998a, p. 7 and Figure 3, p. 9) suggest that in India, during the ten year period since 1986–7, an increase in the central government's fiscal deficit (inclusive of oil pool deficit) by one per cent of GDP reduced private investment by one percent of GDP. Thus fiscal deficits *crowded out* private investment in the last ten years. There is clearly a case for cutting public expenditures on activities that are better left to the private sector. When deficits are financed by increasing public debt, a potential debt-trap can arise if the interest rate on debt exceeds the rate of growth of GDP, as debt service payments would outstrip output growth. We are not there yet, but the possibility is there.

There have been several thorough analyses of India's fiscal situation, notably by Joshi and Little (1994, 1996a, 1996b), Buiter and Patel (1992, 1996, 1997), Burgess and Stern (1993, 1994), Burgess, Howes and Stern (1993) and, above all, by the Chelliah Committee (Ministry of Finance 1992) on tax reforms.

[1] These percentages are based on the old series of GDP (1980–1 as base). The new series of GDP has 1993–4 as base. Using the new series, the central government's fiscal deficits are estimated to be: 1990–1: 7.1 per cent; 1991–2: 5.4 per cent; 1992–3: 5.2 per cent; 1993–4: 6.9 per cent; 1994–5: 5.6 per cent; 1995–6: 4.9 per cent; 1996–7: 4.7 per cent; 1997–8: 5.5 per cent and 1998–9: 5.1 per cent (Government of India 1999, Table 2.1).

I will highlight and update their insights on a few selected topics, including state finances, tax reform, disinvestment, and reduction of subsidies.

Without elaborating on our complex centre–state fiscal set-up, it suffices to recapitulate its main features. The constitution lays down the taxation powers of the centre and states. Roughly, the states can tax land, agricultural income, and sales and impose excise taxes on alcohol while the centre collects taxes on personal and corporation income, wealth, foreign trade, and also excise. The constitution requires the centre to share the revenue from certain taxes in proportions recommended by the Finance Commission, which the President is constitutionally required to appoint every five years. In addition to the transfers arising from the recommendations of the Finance Commission, the Planning Commission, a non-statutory body established by a resolution of Parliament, makes transfers for financing approved outlays of the state on their annual development plans.

It will be generally agreed that the centre has the responsibility to provide crucial public goods such as defence and a common currency. Also given the diversity in the state of development of our states, the centre has a redistributive role in making transfers to the poorer states. The states have been assigned large responsibilities in crucial sectors such as education, health, irrigation, and other investment in agricultural development. Naturally, they cannot discharge these responsibilities adequately if they cannot generate the required resources. Having said this, I must hasten to add that, in practice, our centre-state tax-transfer system has had some disincentive and efficiency reducing effects. The centre's efforts in collecting taxes, such as the income tax, the revenues from which have to be shared with the states, are likely to be less vigorous as compared to taxes such as customs which accrue entirely to the centre. By the same token, if the transfers received from the centre form a large part of its expenditure, and these transfers have no relationship to its own efforts to raise resources, clearly a state is unlikely to be diligent in raising resources. The approach of the first eight Finance Commissions was to fill the gap between the revenues and expenditures of the states and completely ignored this strong disincentive effect.

The states have the right to impose sales taxes, a right which extends to sales to buyers in other states. Obviously an interstate sales tax is a tax on the exports of one state to another. Such taxes prevent India from being a common market and consumers from reaping the static and dynamic efficiency gains of a large market. Unless a state has a national monopoly over a commodity that is competitively produced within its border, a case that is extremely unlikely to arise, it hurts itself by taxing its exports to other states. Even when a state has monopoly power, its exercise will be at the expense of consumers in other states, restricting commerce, and inviting retaliation by other states. In the end consumers in all states are likely to lose. Apart from sales tax competition, after the recent reforms, states have begun to compete with each other to attract private investment by offering tax concessions. This is not healthy either—such competition might end up transferring resources from taxpayers to investors without affecting their location decision. These elementary facts do not seem to have been understood by most state governments.

The states are constitutionally barred from borrowing in international financial markets and need the centre's consent for any borrowing in the domestic market, if they are indebted to the centre or have an outstanding loan guaranteed by the centre. Since all states are indebted to the centre, this constraint is binding on all of them. The states share in the central government's borrowing from captive sources of finance such as banks, insurance companies, and non-government pension and provident funds which are required to be invested in designated government securities. Of course the states cannot directly monetize any part of their deficits.

It would seem that these restrictions impose a hard budget constraint on states. But, in fact, the states have succeeded in getting around them by diverting resources meant for investments to current expenditure, and indirect borrowing, for example, by running up arrears with PSEs (for example, state electricity boards (SEBs) have been tardy in paying their dues to Coal India and the National Thermal Power Corporation (NTPC)). This in turn has led the centre and PSEs to impose restrictions—Coal India now has a cash and carry policy and the central government has chosen to retain up to 15 per cent of the transfers due to the states to clear the SEBs arrears with the NTPC.

The perverse incentives created by the Planning Commission in financing the capital and operating costs of new (centrally sponsored) state projects included in the plan for five years should be noted. States are thus encouraged to attract such projects but once the centre ceases to pay for the operating costs, their incentives to run the projects wane. Also, since all states pay the same rate of interest on loans from the central government, they feel no market pressure to maintain credit worthiness. The net result of all this is that the gross fiscal deficit of the states has fluctuated between 2.7 per cent to 3.4 per cent of GDP since the 1980s with no downward trend—indeed in the three fiscal years including 1997–8, the ratios have been between 3.1 per cent and 3.4 per cent (World Bank 1997, Table 2.2 and World Bank 1998a, Figure 1).

Under the present system, the states have established a large infrastructure and spent on social services, including many populist programmes, without adequate financing through taxes or recovery of costs from users of state-provided goods and services. In the context of electoral politics as practised in India, populism is attractive to politicians of all shades. State payrolls have expanded to the point that a substantial part of their revenues are spent on wages and salaries alone. The states also have to match any largesse, such as the recent pay hikes, conferred by the centre on its employees or face   disruptive agitations.

The economic reforms of 1991 have radically altered the options open to the states—they can now compete for private capital to infrastructural sectors which were earlier financed entirely by the government. But the states will be unable to attract private capital without good quality infrastructure, particularly power and roads, an educated labour force, and efficient, business-friendly bureaucracy. Improvement in the quality and an increase in the quantity of infrastructural services depend on reforms of the operation, pricing, and regulation of the PSEs as well as on additional investment that would require substantial resources. Both for sending the appropriate signals to users and for raising resources for investment, the states will have to address pricing issues with respect to electricity, irrigation, water, education, and other goods and services provided by the government. It is disquieting that as many as seven states decreased their spending during 1990–6 on both economic and social infrastructure. Only one state, Rajasthan, either maintained or increased its spending on both. Some states, notably Andhra

Pradesh, Gujarat, Haryana, Orissa, and Rajasthan have initiated reforms in their power sector. The reform process has to be expanded to include other states and other areas besides power, deepened, and accelerated to restore fiscal stability to the states. The task of reforming the complex set of taxes, direct and indirect, at the centre and states is a challenging and daunting task; the contours of needed reforms are well known and have been discussed in the several studies I mentioned earlier, as well as by the Chelliah Committee (Ministry of Finance 1992). As a proportion of GDP, direct taxes hit a low of 2.3 per cent in 1990–1, falling below the share of customs duties. The proportion of direct taxes in total taxes has fallen steeply from 40 per cent in the 1950s to 31 per cent in the budget estimates for 1998–9. Some measures have been announced in the central budget for 1998–9, to expand the tax base by identifying potential tax payers through several presumptive criteria. At the same time, the budget raised the income tax exemption limits that are already high relative to per capita income. While there may be good administrative reasons for this step, nonetheless it has the undesirable consequence of reducing the tax base. Land tax as a source of revenue has virtually disappeared and agricultural incomes remain largely outside the tax net. Replacing the existing set of indirect taxes through a system of value added taxes has not made rapid progress. Issues such as whether, by amending the constitution if necessary, we should let the centre levy the value added tax (VAT) and share the revenues with the states, or whether the VAT should be completely in state hands with each state choosing its own rates, coverage, and exemptions, are yet to be discussed extensively, let alone resolved.

I have long felt that the centre's roles should be confined to national defence, external relations, the maintenance of national networks of communications and transport and a common currency, and ensuring that there is a single, that is national, common market. To these I would also add a relatively circumscribed role of redistribution across states. All other activities belong to the states. It is possible that, with relatively little mobility of factors across states, such a scheme might either accentuate the existing interstate disparities, or alternatively it might in fact encourage states to compete for providing an environment that is most conducive to economic and social development. I am optimistic that it would be the latter, and as such, interstate competition in tax rates and provision and pricing of infrastructural services will in fact be a race-to-the-top rather than a race-to-the-bottom.

Let me turn to public enterprise reform from a fiscal perspective. Far from being engines of growth, PSEs have been a major burden on our public finances. As I discussed in the first lecture, the progress in divestment has been painfully slow. The Disinvestment Commission has so far submitted eight reports covering forty-three public sector undertakings (PSUs) and ten more PSEs have been referred to the commission in November 1998. The commission has recommended the sale of some PSUs on an as-is-where-is basis. Yet the government has apparently not proceeded very far in implementing the recommendation. The government has also chosen to exclude the commission from the process of monitoring and supervising the disinvestment thereby curtailing its powers. What is needed is not a toothless disinvestment commission but one which has the statutory authority to implement its considered recommendations. We are not moving in that direction.

One key issue is the disposition of the proceeds from the sale of assets of the public sector. One suggestion is to use the sale proceeds to reduce liabilities of the public sector, viz. public debt, rather than the fiscal deficit. Of course, funds are fungible, and *if the government allocated its resources efficiently*, the opportunity cost of funds at the margin would be the same in all uses. As such it would be a matter of indifference whether disinvestment proceeds are used to reduce the debt or the deficit. But this is a big if. In the real world, governments are not necessarily rational and efficient allocators of funds, and the Indian government is no exception. As such, reducing debt, rather than fiscal deficits, with disinvestment proceeds could indeed be a better option as it would add to the pressure on the government for reducing the fiscal deficit.

The economic and social rationales for a number of explicit and implicit budgetary subsidies of the central and state governments are weak or non-existent. The well known report of the National Institute of Public Finance and Policy (Government of India 1997) estimated that the explicit and implicit subsidies of the government were as high as 14.4 per cent of the GDP in

1994-5 of which *three-fourths* or 10.7 per cent of the GDP were on *non-merit goods* (that is goods that neither generated significant and positive externalities nor were of importance from the perspective of poverty alleviation). In any case, as discussed in Chapter 3, even subsidies, such as food subsidies, that are rationalized on grounds of poverty alleviation, are neither well-targeted nor cost-effective. The scope for reducing fiscal deficits through reduction, if not elimination, of socially unnecessary subsidies and elimination of costly and ineffective programmes is substantial.

5

Education and Health

In rhetoric, though emphatically not in reality, the education and health sectors have always been accorded very high priority in India. For example, in 1938 Pandit Nehru's National Planning Committee set what it called an objective test for improvement in nutrition, namely the attainment of a balanced diet having a caloric value of 2,400–2,800 kilo calories per day per adult worker. The committee also suggested indices of progress including liquidation of illiteracy, increase in the average expectation of life, and the provision of medical facilities on the basis of one unit per hundred population (Nehru 1946, pp. 401–3). The People's Plan of the Indian Federation of Labour stated that 'the object of the planned economy must be to provide for the satisfaction of the immediate and basic needs of the Indian people within a period of ten years. These are in respect of food, clothing, shelter, health and education' (Banerjee et al. 1944, pp. 3–8). The Bombay Plan of businessmen had 'the modest aim of securing a general standard of living which would leave a reasonable margin over the minimum requirements of human life' (Thakurdas et al. 1944, p. 29). They defined these minimum requirements as a balanced diet of 2,800 kilo calories per day, clothing and housing needs at 30 yards and at least 100 square feet per person respectively, and some provision for education and health. What is more they were emphatic 'that every person above the age of 10 should be able to read, write and to take intelligent interest in private and social life is yet another of the constituents of a minimum standard of living' (Thakurdas et al. 1944, p. 29). In his famous and stirring 'tyrst with destiny' speech on the eve of independence on 15 August 1947, Pandit Nehru reminded the country that the task ahead included 'the ending of poverty and

ignorance and disease and inequality of opportunity' (as repro-
duced in Gopal 1984, pp. 76–7).

The Constitution of India, adopted in 1950 by the Constituent
Assembly, included an important chapter on Directive Principles
of State Policy. Although the provisions of this chapter are not
enforceable through the courts, nonetheless they clearly indicate
what the framers of the constitution expected the state to do.
Article 41 required the state to endeavour to provide 'for security
of the right to work, to education, and to public assistance in
cases of unemployment, old age, sickness and disablement and in
other cases of undeserved want' (Basu 1994, p. 322). Article 45
enjoined the state to 'endeavor to provide within a period of ten
years from the commencement of this constitution, for free and
compulsory education for all children until they complete the age
of 14' (ibid., p. 324). Article 47 required that 'the state shall
regard raising of the level of nutrition and standard of living of
its people and the improvement of public health as among its
primary duties' (ibid., p. 325).

The Parliamentary resolution of 1950 that established the
Planning Commission, set the commission the task of 'translating
the goals of social and economic policy prescribed in the Directive
Principles of the Constitution . . . into a national programme
based upon the assessment of needs and resources' (Srinivasan
1992, pp. 116–7). Every Five Year Plan document since the first
in 1951 has continued to stress the priority of education and
health.

The reality in contrast to the soaring rhetoric is sobering.
General living standards have certainly improved—since independence, life expectancy at birth has nearly doubled, literacy
rate of the population above the age of five years has tripled, and
per capita availability of food and clothing have increased
significantly. But these achievements have been modest, not only
in comparison with the goals and aspirations of the people at the
dawn of independence and earlier, but even more so in
comparison with what many other developing countries of Asia
and some in Africa have achieved. The fact that even within India
the achievements of some states, such as Kerala in education,
health, and life expectancy, compare favourably with those of
countries with much higher levels of income is a sad commentary
on the failure of other states and the country as a whole.

The fact of India's failure is accepted by all, but there is much less of a consensus on the blame or cause for this failure. For example, Drèze and Sen (1995), while conceding that there is considerable truth in the diagnosis that the blame could be put on the insufficient development of market incentives in India, argue that it is not the only cause. They suggest that 'there are many failures, particularly in the development of public educational facilities, health care provisions, social security arrangements, local democracy, environmental protection and so on, and stifling of market incentives is one part of that larger picture' (Drèze and Sen 1995, p. 8). As Jagdish Bhagwati (1998) remarks in his review of the work of Drèze and Sen, the authors had apparently ignored the long-standing and informed debate in India of the failures listed by them when they flippantly assert

Debates on such questions as the details of tax concessions to be given to multinationals, or whether Indians should drink Coca Cola, or whether the private sector should be allowed to operate city buses, tend to 'crowd out' the time that is left to discuss the abysmal situation of basic education and elementary health care, or the persistence of debilitating social inequalities or other issues that have a crucial bearing on the well-being and freedoms of the population'. [Drèze and Sen 1995, p. vii]

I would also endorse the two other points made by Bhagwati: the first, and foremost, had the market incentives not been stifled, including with respect to access to international markets, India's growth in the last five decades would not only have been considerably faster but also would have benefited the poor significantly. This would have meant that the poor would have had more resources of their own to spend on health and education and the government also would have had more resources to spend on these activities. The second point is that the root cause for the stifling of market incentives and for the several failures listed by Sen and Drèze is the same, namely the pursuit of a development strategy that gave a central role to state-directed, state-controlled, import-substituting, and capital-intensive industrialization, in general, and the development of heavy industries, in particular. The licence-permit-raj that executed this development strategy became a cancerous growth on the economy and body politic and failed to deliver growth and social justice.

The economic reforms initiated by Dr Manmohan Singh in 1991 represent a watershed. They were not merely liberalization of some of the more irksome aspects of the licence-permit-raj, as they had been, in the last years of Mrs. Gandhi and Rajiv Gandhi's tenure. The Manmohan Singh reforms went beyond and were based on the recognition that the development strategy needed to be altered and this required systemic change and not just tinkering here and there. Unfortunately the reform process has not smoothly gone forward beyond the abolition of the licence-permit-raj with respect to investment and import licensing, reducing tariffs and removing quotas on non-consumer good imports, opening up some sectors for domestic and foreign investment, and some hesitant and limited moves to disinvest equity in Public Sector Enterprises. The process, in fact, is stalled and the politically difficult decisions with respect to privatization, like opening up the insurance sector to the private sector, and reform of the banking sector, labour, and bankruptcy laws are yet to be made. Two important sectors, namely, the agriculture and social sectors, have largely been left out of the reform process.

This is unfortunate for two reasons. First of all, a population and a labour force that are either largely illiterate or have minimal education, and that are subject to debilitating illnesses, invariably limit the benefits from the reforms in other sectors. Secondly, as is rightly stressed by Drèze and Sen, education and health are valuable achievements in themselves and are also instrumental in enhancing an individual's effective freedom. We cannot any longer afford to exclude health and education from the reform agenda. They have to become an integral part of it.

Let me first describe the dimensions of the problem, first in education and then in health, before discussing possible reforms. It is well established that the allocation of resources, public and private, to primary and secondary education in India has been inadequate, even though private and social returns to these stages of education are high. Relatively more resources have been devoted to higher education in India compared to other developing countries, for example, China. The consequences of this misallocation of resources have been extremely serious for the poor in general, and female children in particular, who depend on public spending to a larger extent than the non-poor to get educated. This is particularly unfortunate, since without access to good schooling and health care facilities, their chances of escaping poverty in their lifetimes are considerably diminished.

It has been estimated that 35 million children between the ages of six and ten years are out of school—their lack of education denies them and the nation of the high returns from primary education such as better family health, smaller family size, and healthier children for educated women.[1] Less than 50 per cent of the children from poor households enrol, and only one in five of those who enrol complete eight years of basic education. This means that the poor, because they either do not enrol or drop out before completing eight years of schooling, do not benefit from public spending on education to the same extent as the non-poor. The wealthy send their children of both sexes to school wherever they live, but there are enormous interstate disparities in enrolment and completion among the poor. Girls from poor households are only one-fifth as likely to complete eight years of schooling as their female counterparts from the well-to-do households.

The proportion of six to fourteen year olds in school from the bottom 40 per cent of the distribution of households by economic status, varies from a low of 37.8 per cent in Bihar to 88.7 per cent in Kerala, whereas in the top 20 per cent of the distribution the variation is much less, from 84.6 per cent in Assam to 96.1 per cent in Kerala. Simulation exercises show that of a cohort of 100 children from the bottom 40 per cent, only 14 complete 8th grade in Rajasthan and West Bengal, while 53 do so in Kerala. A staggering 64 do not enrol in school or drop out before completing their first grade in Bihar and 62 drop out in Andhra Pradesh, while only 6 drop out in Kerala. Among the top 20 per cent of the rich households, there is considerably less variation in completion and drop-outs—drop-outs vary from 9 in West Bengal to 1 in Kerala while completion rates vary from 67 in Meghalaya to 92 in Kerala.

The differences between the sexes also narrow as incomes rise. In rural India, the average odds of a girl being enroled is 0.66 as opposed to 0.75 for a boy in the poorest quintile, while the odds are respectively 1.31 and 1.23 respectively for the richest quintile.

---

[1] I have drawn on World Bank (1998b) for the data and analysis in what follows.

Interestingly, the marginal odds, that is the probability of enrolment if the average enrolment in the rural population as a whole were to rise by a percentage point, is almost equal for girls and boys in the poorest quintile at 1.08 and 1.09 respectively. This has the implication that subsidies to primary education, that raise the average enrolment rates, are not only pro-poor but also have no bias against female children. Although sex differences in enrolment and educational attainments drop as household incomes rise, the pro-boy bias seems to be the result of a deeper social phenomenon. For example, in parts of the southern state of Tamil Nadu which has high literacy rates for both males and females, female infanticide and foeticide are as common as they are in the northern state of Rajasthan which has low literacy rates for both sexes.

The analysis of the determinants of the differences in enrolment and drop-out rates across states and income groups suggests that state poverty alone does not explain these gaps—for example, Tamil Nadu and Himachal Pradesh have higher poverty rates than Andhra Pradesh but Andhra Pradesh fares much worse than the other two in educational attainment. Of course, both demand factors, such as household characteristics and behaviours, as well as supply factors affect the outcomes. Interestingly, whether or not a primary or secondary school is present in a village has no significant effect on enrolments, except in a few states. This is probably because school quality in terms of teacher absenteeism, availability of blackboards, and teaching aids matter much more than the presence of school. Also important is the distance of the village school from the location of homesteads of the poor, particularly of the Scheduled Castes. A survey of low-literacy districts in eight states found that schools with a high concentration of Scheduled Tribe students are of a poorer quality—more of them located in *kuccha* buildings, with less furniture, fewer teachers with recent training, etc.

This sad story of the relative neglect of primary education and its disproportionate deleterious consequences for the poor children, particularly girls, clearly suggest the urgent tasks ahead: first, the access to schools, their quality, and efficiency have to be improved by, on the one hand, influencing the demand factors, such as household income, and also the supply factors focusing on school quality. Reducing gaps in enrolment, improving teacher performance, and enhancing the quality of books and the management of schools are important. Local community participation in monitoring school management and performance has to be fostered—the experience of Madhya Pradesh in devolving primary schooling management to Panchayati Raj Institutions and its innovative education guarantee scheme is very encouraging in this regard. Above all, spending on primary education has to be increased with the central government contributing a significant share. In the District Primary Education Programme (DPEP), the Government of India provides grants to the equivalent of 85 per cent of the cost of approved investment by the states. It would be appropriate to concentrate on the states of Andhra Pradesh, Bihar, Madhya Pradesh, Orissa, Uttar Pradesh, and West Bengal, which considerably lag behind others in performance. Based on the DPEP experience, the World Bank estimates the total cost, inclusive of the cost of building, teachers' salaries, books etc., that must be incurred to provide a reasonable quality of education for all children aged six to ten years by year 2007 to be around Rs. 19,500 crores at 1993 prices (World Bank 1998b, Box 2.2, p. 19). The Bank suggests that this sum can be raised if the budgetary allocation to education goes up from 3.7 per cent of GDP now to 6 per cent by 2002 and remains constant thereafter and the economy grows at the rate of 5 per cent or more. The task therefore is not unmanageable. Careful decentralization to ensure that existing disparities across states and within states are not exacerbated, while reaping the benefits of monitoring that is closer to the communities involved will pay rich dividends.

Turning now to health, as the experience of Tamil Nadu shows, there is synergy between health, nutrition, and schooling. It should cause no surprise that the poor suffer disproportionately from illnesses, diseases, and their consequences. Their infant, child, and maternal mortality rates are much higher than those of the non-poor. Rates of child malnutrition are higher as well. Although life expectancy has doubled since independence, and the infant mortality rate has halved, child mortality in India is still one of the highest in the world. Communicable diseases and perinatal and maternal mortality account for 12.5 per cent of the deaths of women in the age group of fifteen to forty-five years— these cause 470 deaths per 100,000 population, a rate four times higher that of China, and 2.5 times higher that of the world as a whole. The incidence of tuberculosis among the poor is 4.5 times higher than among the rich, 3.2 times higher for malaria, 2.8 times higher for leprosy, and so on.

The rich–poor gap in the incidence of communicable diseases is much higher than of non-communicable diseases. To start with, the poor have a shorter life span. Also, epidemics kill the poor at disproportionately high rates. Infectious diseases are the bane of the poor. As such, public expenditures that are targeted at preventing and dealing with communicable diseases will benefit the poor disproportionately. Besides, since the externalities from such diseases are significant, targeting them would be socially desirable from this perspective as well.

In analysing the determinants of the health status of individuals and groups, it is useful to go beyond variables such as income, occupation, location, and personal characteristics and examine factors related to policies in non-health sectors. These would include policies relating to the provison of education and physical infrastructure, public goods such as water, sanitation, and vaccinations, and lastly, health-policy related factors such as access to health centres, hospitals, and other publicly provided services. The findings from an econometric analysis of the data on child mortality from the National Family Health survey of 1992–3 are: children of Scheduled Caste and young mothers are more likely to die before the age of two years. Interestingly this does not hold for children of Scheduled Tribe mothers. When one controls for income, education, public infrastructure, etc. the states which do better than expected are Goa, Manipur, Mizoram, and Nagaland. But one has to be careful not to over-interpret these results. Public policies in sectors such as education, particularly female education, do have significant effects in reducing child mortality. While the presence of a Public Health Centre is found to have no significant effect, the presence of a sub-centre has a puzzling negative effect on survival. Not surprisingly, the lack of immunization has a strong negative effect on survival while privately accessible water, presumably of better purity, significantly improves survival.

It goes without saying that the objective of achieving a healthy and literate population is of high intrinsic value. But its instrumental value in enabling the attainment of a more rapid and egalitarian growth is significant as well. There is no doubt that since independence we have not allocated adequate resources to education and health. Even the limited resources that were allocated were not efficiently and equitably spent. Reforms to remedy this double-failure are urgently needed.

6

Infrastructure

The establishment and existence of a well functioning and efficient basic infrastructure, such as power, telecommunications and transport, and water (for human and industrial use as well as for irrigation and sanitation and hygiene), is essential for economic development and growth. This fact was evident to the pioneers of development thinking who used the phrase 'social overhead capital' to describe these activities. The phrase 'social and economic infrastructure' is of more recent vintage, and includes not only physical infrastructure but also networks of social institutions, particularly informal ones. Coleman, a sociologist, coined the phrase 'social capital' to denote such networks and the political scientist Robert Putnam has popularized its use.

Certain aspects of the infrastructural activities distinguish them from other economic activities. First, they involve relatively large and lumpy investments. Second, for several reasons, including lumpiness of investments, there are likely to be significant economies of scale in many of them. Third, there are significant externalities in infrastructure, such as network externalities in telecommunication and transport networks, environmental externalities in the case of power generation activities, externalities in the form of prevention of communicable diseases in the case of investment in water supply systems, sewerage, and waste disposal, etc. Fourth, some of the infrastructural services are like public goods, that is they are non-rival and non-excludable in their use. Fifth, often there are several distinguishable categories of users of infrastructural services. To cite a few examples: in rail and other transportation, passenger services can be distinguished from cargo or freight services; within each class of service a further distinction, such as between suburban, local, and long distance transportation, can be made as well. In telephone services local calls are distinguished from national and international trunk calls and so on. In India, in pricing of electric power household consumers, agriculturalists, and commercial industrial users have been distinguished. The same basic plant and equipment are used to provide several categories of services, giving rise to issues relating to the cross-subsidization of one or more category of users by others.

These several aspects imply that a competitive market system is unlikely to provide a socially optimal level of most of the infrastructural services. Indeed because of extensive scale economies and the large size of investment required, some, though certainly not all, of these activities have the characteristics of natural monopolies. While market failure calls for corrective action if the benefits from such action exceed costs, there is a wide spectrum of choices in the type of action. For example, a service that is a natural monopoly can be produced either by a state (or corporatized public) or private enterprise within a regulatory framework established by the state. In some cases, production, transportation or transmission, and delivery to the ultimate user could all be vertically integrated into one state-run or state–regulated private monopoly. In other cases, some segments, such as production and distribution, could be served by competitive private enterprises, while transportation or distribution could remain a monopoly. There are also a number of choices in the regulatory framework, if regulation is chosen: for a large economy, should there be a single agency to regulate an activity for the economy as a whole or should there be several, possibly regional agencies? In sectors like telecommunications, a multinational regulatory agency is also a possibility. There are a whole host of issues about the mechanism of regulation. Different forms of organization, production, transportation, and distribution as well as regulation have efficiency and equity implications.

In the early development literature the presumption was overwhelmingly in favour of a vertically integrated state monopoly in the production, transportation, and delivery of most infrastructural services. And many developing countries chose that option. In our country, since independence, railways have remained a departmentally run state monopoly. Until recently, telephone and telecommunications and air transportation were state monopolies and, with a few exceptions, so were power generation, transmission, and distribution.

Paul Joskow (1999) points out that historically the performance of state enterprises in providing infrastructural services has been quite poor. In many countries much of the population does not have access to these services at all, as has been the case for our rural population with respect to telecommunications and even electricity for a long time. Some are lucky enough to gain access only after waiting for many years in a queue, but more often than not, most had to pay bribes or use influence, as was common in India for telephone and electricity connections. The quality of service is poor in many developing countries including India, with high rates of equipment outages, fluctuating voltages, and interruptions of supply. The enterprises usually employ many more people than needed for their efficient functioning so that productivity is low. Those employed usually enjoy much higher wages and perquisites than similar workers elsewhere in the economy. Again, in India, as in many other developing countries, prices charged for infrastructural services do not even cover the variable costs of their supply, let alone contribute to fixed costs.[1] Needless to say they do not generate surpluses to finance investment. Above all, the process of staffing, particularly of the appointment of the executive officers who are to manage these enterprises, has been used by the bureaucracy to capture senior positions for themselves. The process of staffing has also become increasingly politicized, non-transparent, and frequently corrupt. The sad performance of enterprises providing infrastructural services has been a factor in the poor performance of many developing countries including India. Thus the case for reforming the infrastructural sectors is very strong, both for improving their own performance and for removing the drag of an unreformed and poorly performing infrastructure sector on the realization of potential benefits of reforms in other sectors. Some of the complexities involved in reforming monopolies and

---

[1] The cost of supply is itself much higher than what it would have been if the service capacity were of an appropriate scale and its provision were to be efficiently managed.

quasi-monopolies have been alluded to in Chapter 1. However, such complexities do not mean that reforms are infeasible, but only that careful prior thought needs to be given before adopting particular reform modes. Our reforms of the telecommunications sector amply illustrates my point.[2] Until recently, the telephone in India was viewed as a luxury consumer service that enables private communication rather than an essential producer service needed to link markets, producers, and consumers. Fortunately, we have moved away from this idea. The annual growth of new telephone connections in different parts of the country is steadily increasing every year but there is still a long way to go before all the Indian villages have access to a public call office at least. According to the World Bank (1996, Box 5.2), there was a waiting list of 2.27 million customers for telephones in 1996 and well over 100,000 villages were without telephone services.

The reform process in telecommunications began with three very important fundamental policy decisions: the number and location of new companies, the use of an auction to grant the licence to operate, and the establishment of the Telecommunications Regulatory Authority of India (TRAI) to regulate the industry, including the prices charged by the incumbent state-owned monopolist. All this was carried out without fully resolving the possible overlap and conflict between TRAI as a regulator and the Ministry of Telecommunications as a policy-maker.

The first decision about the number and location of private companies meant that regardless of the success of the entrants, the industry would be unlikely to develop in a manner that was in the interests of users of the telephone system. By preventing entrants from offering long-distance service and by deciding the boundaries of each metro and circle system, the government imposed a configuration on the industry that should have been determined by the cost of service and the relative intensity of demand. The opportunities for creating a seamless national wireless network, which incidentally would have reduced the cost and increased the

[2] The paragraphs on reforms of telecommunications are taken from my article, with Professor Roger Noll of Stanford University, entitled 'Revisiting Indian Telecom Reform' and published in *Business Standard*, Delhi, 21 August 1999.

attractiveness to private firms of extending service into less populous cities and regions, remained unutilized. The possibility that, in at least some parts of the nation, true competition would emerge among multiple carriers remained ignored and untested. The second decision, to auction the licences, seems to have been solely for the purpose of generating a short-term financial windfall to the treasury. The policy that maximizes the revenues from an auction involves the creation of a monopoly. In wireless telephony there is absolutely no reason to pursue this course, for the technology does not have significant economies of scale. Hence, the only conceivable reason to limit to one the number of entrants in an area is to extract monopoly profits from consumers, and then through an auction transfer those monopoly profits back to the government.

Once it is recognized that wireless telephony does not have the characteristics of a natural monopoly, it should be obvious that by creating a monopoly and capturing all or part of the monopoly rents by charging a licence fee, the government is merely substituting a non-tax instrument, viz. the licence fee, for tax instruments for raising revenues. Hence, the issue is poorly formulated as to whether the industry received a bail-out. Instead, the proper formulation is as an issue in public finance: did the auction set an implicit tax on telecommunications that was so high that it both impeded the growth of the industry and actually collected less revenues than might have been collected if the tax were lower?

The best decision in the reform process was to create TRAI, a regulatory authority that has managers with impeccable reputations and which was intended to be truly independent. However, since the Department of Telecommunications (DoT) was the policy-maker while it still retained its service-providing units subject to TRAI's regulatory authority, conflict between TRAI and DoT became inevitable. Such a conflict raised doubts about whether the government intended TRAI to be truly independent. For Indian telephony to grow and be efficient, someone has to set the right prices in uncompetitive markets and manage the process by which companies interconnect with each other, so that multiple systems can operate efficiently as a single national telecommunications network. A respected, independent regulator is necessary to absorb and deflect all of the short-term political heat that naturally is created from making the tough decisions that must be made to get the telecommunications system on the right track. Reversing the decision of the regulator should be possible—to retain its democratic legitimacy—but reversal should require a lengthy and transparent process, such as winning a battle in court or passing new legislation. The reason is quite simple: the regulatory rules under which the industry operates must be seen as durable, predictable, and transparent if the private industry is going to be induced to invest billions of rupees to expand and improve service.

Unfortunately, events show that the Ministry of Tele-communications and the Prime Minister's Office (PMO) retain too much authority to meddle by means of short-term, opaque tinkering with policy. The problem has little to do with whether political tinkering, on average, improves policy, but the mere fact that tinkering, however nobly motivated, constantly makes policy uncertain and a matter for constant political negotiation. In the present regime, nothing is ever decided, and all decisions are provisional because they are constantly up for revision. This problem will not go away with an election and a new government.

So what should be done to salvage matters? First, there is really no point in deciding anything before the election that does not have support from across the political spectrum, for whatever is decided now will be revisited as soon as the new government is inaugurated. Second, the decisions to limit entry with respect to location and type of service should be rescinded. All of the Indian telecommunications sectors should immediately be opened to entry, and integrated companies that provide all services throughout the nation should be encouraged rather than pro-hibited. Third, the obligation to pay the licence fees should be largely rescinded, in part because the government should change the basis of the deal by allowing more competition and national firms. But this does not mean that the government should abandon the idea that telecommunications, or any other major infrastructure industry, should be a significant source of tax revenues. Thus, fourth, the government should adopt a significant sales tax—or revenue-sharing arrangement—for all carriers, covering all services, with one exception. Namely, fifth, to prevent the sales tax from being regressive, the government should set a lower tax (perhaps even zero) on calls from pay telephones. Sixth, to terminate the endless battles between TRAI and the Ministry of Telecommunications, legislation should be passed that unequivocally gives all rate-making, standard-setting, and licensing powers to TRAI, and the corporatization, if not full privatization, of the state-owned carrier should be completed as soon as possible.

Joskow points out, as infrastructure sectors are privatized and restructured to promote competition in potentially competitive segments, the creation of supporting regulatory institutions, as an integral part of the whole reform programme and not as an afterthought, is vital. What is more, not enough attention has been devoted in India to the creation and design of regulatory institutions. Other than the Securities and Exchanges Board of India (SEBI) which regulates the financial markets, only two, TRAI and Tariff Authority for Major Ports (TAMP) have been set up. In the power sector, the Parliament has enacted a law enabling the states to establish State Electricity Regulatory Commissions (SERCs). Several states have either set up the SERCs or are in the process of setting them up. With respect to roads and irrigation, we have barely begun to allow the private sector to participate in investment in roads and farmers to get involved in the operation of the irrigation system. As is evident from the experience of TRAI and SEBI, problems regarding the autonomy of regulatory agencies have already arisen and need to be addressed.

In Chapter 1, I discussed the regulatory issues analysed by Joskow in some detail and will not repeat them here. Instead I will make a few remarks on some of our crippling infrastructural problems. Let me begin with the power sector. According to the latest economic survey (Government of India 1999, Table 9.4), the total gross subsidy on the sale of power in 1997–8 was a staggering Rs. 245 billion of which Rs. 191 billion were due to subsidized sale to the agricultural sector. Total gross subsidy and the subsidy to agriculture are projected to rise to Rs. 316 billion and 238 billion in 1999–2000 (ibid., Table 9.4). As against a 3 per cent rate of return on their net fixed assets in service, stipulated in the Electricity Supply Act of 1948 and which became operative in 1985, only in four SEBs the actual rate of return in 1996–7 exceeds 3 per cent, with subsidy. Starting with Orissa, five other states, namely Andhra Pradesh, Gujarat, Haryana,

Uttar Pradesh, and Rajasthan have begun the reform process in this vital sector. These states have endorsed the creation of an independent regulatory agency for power, approved the principle that tariffs should reflect costs, agreed to divest their shares in power generating companies and to encourage competition among independent power producers, and, finally, to privatize the distribution function of the state electricity boards. While these decisions by the five states are to be welcomed, and the substantial progress made by Orissa is encouraging, it is still too early to say whether all the steps in the reform process will be successfully implemented in these states, let alone other states which may follow. As the World Bank (1996, p. 96) notes:

the fundamental obstacle to private sector investment in the power sector is the weak financial position of the State Electricity Boards (SEBs) which operate virtually all the country's distribution networks through which the power supplied by potential private investors have to be sold (emphasis in the original).

But for the weak financial position of the SEBs and the consequent uncertainty of their being paid, private investors would not need counter-guarantees by the central government before they invest. It is encouraging that competitive bidding has been made mandatory for new private power projects. With a transparent bidding process that is backed up by adequate technical and economic preparation, the best price and quality projects would be the winners.

In the transportation sector, because of the poor performance of the railways, over time there has been a shift in long distance cargo transportation from railways to private lorries. Poor enforcement of rules of overloading has allowed lorries to exceed their axle-load limit which in part contributes to the poor state of Indian roads. With the passing of the National Highways Amendments Act in 1995, private sector investment in the construction, operation, and maintenance of national highways is now possible. The National Highway Authority of India and the Ministry of Surface Transport have also taken several steps, including tax holidays, acquisition and transfer of land to the private investor, improved access to finance and speedier clearance from state governments, to encourage private investment in build-operate-transfer (BOT) projects. As yet only the construction of a 20 km bypass near Mumbai has been completed under this arrangement. The BOT approach is being extended to airport construction and to railways in the form of build-own-lease-transfer schemes for railway assets such as rolling stock and electrified lines. However, that all is not smooth sailing is seen from the tortuous history of the failure of the attempted private sector involvement in the construction of a new airport in Bangalore.

In civil aviation, the government-owned Air India faces competition from other international carriers and has been making significant losses. India Airlines faces some limited competition. The unconscionable delay in deciding on the Tata–Singapore Airlines proposal to enter domestic aviation led to its withdrawal by the proposers. This is not a good sign.

The average ship turnaround time in 1996–7 was 7.8 days—it was even higher, 8.1 days, in 1990–1 (Government of India 1998, p. 132). Compared to Singapore's port where the turnaround time is a few hours, rather than several days, and other ports in the Asian region, Indian ports are abysmally inefficient.

The reasons for this sorry state of affairs are not too far to seek. According to Peters (1997):

India's ports were originally designed to handle specific categories of traffic which have declined over time while other types of traffic have gained importance. But the ports' berth configurations were not adjusted to the categories of cargo which grew most. In almost all ports productivity levels are extremely low by international standards. Documentary procedures related to cargo handling . . . are extremely complicated. Land-side port access facilities and arrangements for moving inbound and outbound cargo are unsatisfactory. [pp. 7–8]

The net result of all this is that some ports (for example, Calcutta) handle much less cargo than they did fifty years ago. In the line trades very few carriers serve India's ports through direct calls which would have meant unacceptably long waiting times. Most general cargo traffic to and out of India takes place through trans-shipment at more efficient ports such as Colombo. The added cost to India's exporters and importers are substantial.

Realizing the urgent need for reforms, the government has invited private interests to finance new port facilities on a BOT basis. There is some welcome move away from the situation described by Peters (1997, p. 8), 'the principal reasons for such inefficiencies lies in the fact that India's ports are still managed like bureaucracies burdened with rules for the employment and dispatch of labour which critically undermine any effort at improving productivity'. Indeed recalcitrant unionized labour is a serious bottleneck to any productivity-raising change at ports, as well as in other public sector entities. There is still a long way to go before India's ports could compete with more efficient ports in the region such as Colombo in Sri Lanka, let alone Singapore.

7

The Financial Sector

The financial sector consists of formal and informal institutions for borrowing and lending financial resources, markets for trading financial instruments such as equities, debentures and their derivatives, and the markets for sharing, shifting, and trading risk, the last consisting primarily of insurance markets amongst others. From the early days of development economics it was recognized that the functions served by the financial sector were extremely important for development and growth. It was also noted that many of the needed financial institutions and markets were absent in countries at an early stage of development, and even those that existed were very imperfect in their operation. Again, as in other areas, the absence of markets and/or their imperfection or failures were seen by early development thinkers as a rationale for state intervention in the financial sector.

The inherent features of a financial transaction are that, first, its *quid* and *quo* will necessarily be separated in time or will occur at different states of nature, and second, there is likely to be asymmetry of information between the parties to the transaction about the events that the transaction covers. These features create situations in which opportunistic behavior is very likely. A number of examples illustrate the problem. In the absence of a relatively inexpensive mechanism for enforcement of loan contracts a lender cannot be sure of being able to collect, without incurring high costs, the money lent when it becomes due. Moreover since money is fungible, the borrower could always, if he wished to do so, put the borrowed resources to uses other than those to which the lender and borrower had agreed upon at the time they were lent. In insurance and other contingent contracts, there are problems of moral hazard and adverse selection. Moral hazard arises when the insuree loses interest in taking actions that reduce the probability of the event against the occurrence of which he has insured himself, as, for example, in the case of a homeowner whose incentive to take actions that will reduce the probability of his house burning down is blunted, once he has fire insurance. Adverse selection arises, for example, if a health insurer cannot distinguish between those who are inherently more risky with respect to contracting particular health hazards than those who are less likely to do so and has to charge the same premium to all. Then only those who know that they run a greater risk will insure so that the risk characteristic of the insured population will be different from that of the general population. A premium rate that will ensure normal profits to the insurer may not exist under situations of severe adverse selection or moral hazard. This, in turn, means that a market for such insurance will not exist.

The problems of moral hazard, adverse selection, or more generally the possibilities of ex-post opportunistic behaviour by one or both parties to a contract may be rationales for state intervention in financial markets. I should add that the problem of opportunism arises in many contexts such as lending by banks, relations between shareholders, and the management of firms. State intervention takes many forms, such as third party enforcement of contracts through the judicial system, prudential regulation of banks and other financial intermediaries, insistence on collateral in loan contracts, deductibles in insurance contracts, controls on terms of lending or borrowing including interest rates charged or received, as well as state ownership of financial institutions.

In India contract law and regulation of interest rates have a long history going back to at least the Arthaśāstra, a fourth century treatise in Sanskrit on statecraft by Kautilāya. It has a whole chapter on this. Kautilāya even recognizes that a premium has to be included in the interest charged if the transaction involved risk. For example, while he stipulates that 1.5 per cent per month should be the legal interest rate on essentially risk free transactions, he allows much higher interest rates on loans that finance risky transactions that involve transportation through forests, across the seas, and so on (Kangle 1972, p. 226).

In more recent times, Pandit Nehru's National Planning Committee of 1938, or at least some members of the committee including Nehru 'hoped to evolve a socialized system of credit. If banks, insurance, etc. were not nationalized, they should at least be under the control of the state, thus leading to a state regulation of capital and credit' (Nehru 1946, p. 404). The choice between outright nationalization and state or social control of banks came to the fore once again in the late 1960s with the Prime Minister Mrs Gandhi, arguing for nationalization and with the Finance Minister, Morarji Desai, for social control. Mrs Gandhi prevailed and nationalized the banks in 1969 and Morarji Desai resigned from the cabinet.

In the early 1970s, Ronald McKinnon (1973) and Edward Shaw (1973) published their seminal work on 'financial repression', a term which they used to describe a system in developing countries in which the government determined who got and gave credit and at what terms. Such control was exercised by one or more of the following ways: the government regulating which financial institutions will be permitted to do business and how they will operate, the government owning banks and other financial intermediaries, and by control over international capital movements. India, until the recent reforms, had all of these. Most commercial banks (with the exception of a few foreign banks and some small banks) and insurance companies were owned by the government, interest rates were controlled, and there were selective credit controls and directed lending to priority sectors. Through the Cash Reserve Ratio and Statutory Liquidity Ratio, the government ensured that more than 50 per cent of the deposits of the commercial banks was invested in government securities. The government further monetized part of its fiscal deficits through the forced sale of ad hoc treasury bills to the Reserve Bank. The nationalized banks as well as the Reserve Bank had little autonomy in decision making. India was no exception in repressing the financial sector—such repression was almost universal in developing countries until recently—but the financial repression in India went further than that in most countries.

Full liberalization of the financial sector involves the following: elimination of credit controls, deregulation of interest rates, ease of entry into the financial sector, full autonomy for banks, permitting private ownership of banks, and liberalization of international capital controls. Of course, full liberalization presumes the existence of a framework for enforcing prudential regulations and an adequate capital base.

McKinnon and Shaw argued that in a repressed financial system, with low interest rates, savings will be discouraged and part of the saving will flow out of the formal financial system that is subject to controls, thus resulting in a less efficient allocation of investments. Also, a low interest rate on loans makes investments with low rates of returns viable and, with some randomness in lending, will result in lowering the average rate of return of the total investment portfolio as well. However, the two authors expected that with financial liberalization savings will rise, investment allocation will be efficient, there will be greater financial deepening and larger savings, and hence larger investments. The result will be greater efficiency in investment and the growth rate will rise as well.

Many of these expectations, but certainly not all, have been borne out in the episodes of financial liberalization that have taken place in developing and developed countries, particularly since the 1980s. One of the early liberalization episodes in the late 1970s in the Southern Cone countries of Latin America failed. This failure has been attributed to an improper sequencing of liberalization, namely that the financial sector was liberalized prior to establishing macroeconomic stability. Analysis of the Southern Cone experience and insights from the theory of distortions and the theory of the second best led to the conventional prescription that prior to financial liberalization, the macroeconomic environment has to be stabilized and reforms in the real sectors, particularly foreign trade, had to be implemented. This would ensure that investment and capital flows triggered by financial liberalization do not flow to those sectors in which returns to investment are artificially high, and that an apparatus is in place for sound prudential supervision. In this prescription liberalization of external capital accounts should come at the very end of the liberalization process.

These conventional prescriptions have not exactly been followed by countries that have liberalized. Also, there have even been arguments *in favour* of some financial repression, for example by Stiglitz (Murdock and Stiglitz, 1993). In situations where income tax evasion is rampant and debt markets are underdeveloped, it is attractive and perhaps even rational for governments to resort to inflation tax. Thus financial repression, by increasing the demand for money, increases the base for inflation tax. Be that as it may, the evidence from liberalization episodes and other analyses suggests the following (Williamson and Mahar 1998):

1. The McKinnon–Shaw hypothesis that financial development contributes to economic growth is broadly supported in cross-country analysis, although some evidence to the contrary was also found in Latin America in the 1970s and 1980s.
2. The evidence on the elasticity of savings and investment rates with respect to interest rates is mixed. This is not surprising, since a rise in the interest rate has income and substitution effects going in opposite directions, and hence the net effect could be positive.
3. There is some evidence that liberalization redirected investment from less to more efficient uses which is again consistent with the hypothesis that financial development promotes growth.
4. The evidence of increased financial depth consequent to liberalization is difficult to establish firmly since the available proxy for depth, viz. M2/GDP, is not an ideal one, and the movement towards greater depth will depend on whether the economy has poorly developed or well-developed financial markets.

One of the early writers who warned that moving from financial repression to full financial liberalization could make countries more susceptible to financial crisis was my late colleague, Carlos Diaz-Alejandro (1985). He proved to be right: almost all the thirty four countries examined by Williamson and Mahar (1998) experienced some form of systemic financial crisis during 1980–97. After 1997, a few of them (Brazil, Indonesia, and Korea) had another crisis. Russia, which was not included in the study, had a crisis in 1999. Of course not all crises were associated with financial liberalization, but Williamson and Mahar (1998) argue that a majority were. They find that while the policy problem is to design a liberalization programme that does not bring with it an increased susceptibility to financial crisis, there are no generally accepted conclusions as to how this can be done, except for the conventional prescription, discussed earlier, that emerged from an analysis of the experience of libralization in the Southern Cone countries. However, Stiglitz (1994) has suggested that a ceiling on deposit rates (a symptom of financial repression!) may be appropriate for a period.

The broad contours of financial sector reforms in India are well known. First, interest rates for loans greater than Rs. 0.2 million are no longer administratively set, although they continue to be administratively set with respect to savings deposits, small savings, non-resident Indian (NRI) deposits, and loans under Rs. 0.2 million. Cash reserve ratios and statutory liquidity ratios, which were as high as 25 per cent and 38.5 per cent respectively prior to 1991, are now 10 per cent and 25 per cent. Since April 1998, banks have been permitted to set interest rates, up to a maximum equal to the prime rate, on loans under Rs. 0.2 million. As of 6 January 1999, the deposit rate ranged between 9 per cent and 11.5 per cent while the prime lending rate ranged between 12.75 per cent and 13 per cent (Government of India 1999, p. 41). Private (domestic and foreign) entrants have been allowed into the banking sector and these accounted for about 17 per cent of bank assets in 1996–7, up from 11.5 per cent in 1991–2 (World Bank 1998a, p. 14). The Reserve Bank has enhanced its regu-latory powers over non-bank financial institutions (NBFI) and has set capital adequacy norms and prudential regulations for NBFI. Above all, regulations on banks regarding income recognition, definition of non-performing assets, and related provisions have been strengthened. But a lot more remains to be done.

It would seem that India has by no means abandoned the 'loan-mela-loan-mafi' political culture that has characterized lending, namely the extension of credit to the politically sensitive groups and condoning their defaults as well as the directed credit to priority sectors. Several government committees have made recommendations on reforms of the financial sector, including a committee chaired by M. Narasimhan for the second time. Also, the Khan Committee for Harmonizing the Role and Operations of Development Finance Institutions and Banks, the Gupta Committee on Rural Credit, and the Tarapore Committee on Capital Account Convertibility have reported. In arriving at their recommendations, these committees have comprehensively examined the issues involved. I am in agreement with many of the recommendations of the second Narasimham Committee. I am glad that they have endorsed the view that others, including myself, have been advocating: namely that capital-adequacy norms have to be judged in relation to the riskiness of the loan portfolio. The committee rightly recommends that we should move towards a norm of 10 per cent, rather than the average Basle norm of 8 per cent. Even 10 per cent may be too low. They point out that there are virtually no markets in India for hedging risks, and rightly suggest that capital adequacy norms should therefore take into account market risks in addition to credit risks. Their proposal for risk weights of various components of bank portfolios, in particular assigning a 5 per cent weight for market risks of government and government approved securities is right on the mark. Their recommendation for tightening the criteria for classification of a loan as non-performing and for income recognition and appraising are also sensible. The committee is absolutely right in insisting that measures are put in place to ensure that new non-performing assets (NPAs) do not arise in the future before banks have cleared up the balance sheets of their existing NPAs through any of the suggested proposals.

In response to the committee's recommendation, the Union Budget for 1998–9 proposed to raise the minimum Capital to Risk-weighted Asset Ratio (CRAR) to 10 per cent from 8 per cent in phases, with the CRAR rising to 9 per cent by 31 March 2000. By 21 March 1998, as many as nineteen out of twenty seven public sector banks had already reached a CRAR exceeding 10 per cent through large scale recapitalization financed by the government. Although in 1997–8 the absolute amount of NPAs increased by 4.8 per cent over 1996–7, their share in total advances came down to 16.0 per cent from 17.8 per cent (Government of India 1999, pp. 42–3).

I was disappointed that the committee did not stick to the recommendation for reducing the scope of directed credit under priority sectors from 40 per cent to 10 per cent while correctly arguing for the total elimination of interest rate subsidies on the loans to priority sectors. The committee has rightly emphasized the urgency of reducing excess employment, ensuring longer tenure for chief executives as well as lateral recruitment and appropriate compensation for the chief executive, etc. The scandalous quality of customer service by the public sector banks has to be addressed, and computerization of operations has to be extended. There should be no further recourse to debt waivers in rural lending.

Let me turn briefly to capital account convertibility, an issue which the Tarapore Committee analysed in depth. In my view, it would be extremely unwise to rush into this for several reasons. Let me just mention two. First, as was argued some time back by Brecher and Alejandro (1977), in a situation of continuing protection of capital-intensive import competing sectors, any foreign capital, particularly foreign direct investment (FDI), that is attracted to protected sectors would be welfare-reducing. Thus, until such protection is removed increased capital inflows, following capital account convertibility, would not be beneficial. Second, unless our macroeconomic situation is brought firmly under control and the banking sector in particular, as well as the financial sector more broadly, are brought into sound shape, augmented capital inflows could be invested inappropriately thus increasing the probability of a financial crisis when such investments fail, as they most likely will. The management capability of banks in their credit operations with the private sector has to be improved. This improvement should include a better understanding of and ability to appraise the risk characteristics of advances to the private sector. Also, the capital requirements have to be increased progressively to at least 10 per cent as recommended by the Narasimham Committee. It is virtually impossible to design a financial system that is at once free of controls and open to external capital inflows and outflows, and is also at the same time completely immune to financial crisis and panics. As is evident from the recent South-East Asian crises and others that preceded it, the probability of a financial crisis is increased by a weak domestic financial sector which has little or no capacity to appraise risks properly, the expectation arising from past experience that the government will not allow any major bank or financial institution to fail, mismatches in the maturity of borrowed funds relative to advances, because of financing long-term loans with funds borrowed on short term, particularly with external funds, and currency mismatches, that is between borrowed funds denominated in foreign currency and loaned funds in domestic currency. Avoiding all these is certainly not politically easy, particularly cutting off popular loans, shutting down weak financial institutions, and taking action early enough.

It is a pity that the bill on insurance sector reforms could not be passed before Parliament was dissolved in April 1999. Related to insurance reforms is the issue of pensions and provident funds. The possibility of moving to a fully funded transferable system and involving some options for investing a small part of the funds in equities ought to be examined. But the issues involved are complex and require a careful examination and discussion before any changes are made. A more important priority arises from the fact that state-supported provisions for retirement are available for only a very small part of the labour force. Extending some form of social security to all the labour force has to be part of the reform agenda. Also, as the Reserve Bank extends its control over non-bank financial intermediaries, it should ensure that there is healthy competition between banks and non-bank financial institutions for providing the best set of financial options for the public. In India, mortgage finance for housing and other real estate is still underdeveloped. This is yet another area for immediate attention. Now that the Urban Land Ceiling Act has been repealed, any rent controls that still remain on the statute books must be repealed as well.

There is complementarity between reforms in the financial and real sectors. Having access to funds for working capital as well as for long-term investment through an efficiently functioning set of financial intermediaries is undoubtedly essential if the reforms in the real sectors are to succeed and for the real sector to grow more rapidly. As such, financial sector reforms are essential to real sector growth. Equally, if the domestic real sector is not reformed, with free capital movements, savers and investors could look outside the home economy for the use of their funds. There is also the danger that the signals for investment emerging from a distorted real sector could be faulty so that investible resources end up in the wrong sectors, even if these are invested at home. Thus, real sector reform is essential if financial sector reform is to bear fruit in terms of more rapid growth.

India is a signatory of the General Agreement on Services as well as the recently concluded Financial Services Agreement, both being offshoots of the Uruguay Round Agreement of multilateral trade negotiations. As such, we need to ensure that our domestic financial sector reforms anticipate what is needed to compete in the emerging liberal world financial order. Also, firms involved in exports and imports would continue to be disadvantaged relative to their foreign competitors if financial services remain inefficient and relatively costly.

8

International Trade and Investment

India's insulation from world markets until the reforms of 1991 stemmed from a long-standing distrust of markets and international trade in general and the fear that greater involvement in foreign trade would inevitably retard India's industrialization. More than six decades ago Sir M. Visveswaraya, asserted that 'India may be an industrially developed country or it may be a market for manufactured goods from outside and not both' (Visveswaraya 1934, pp. 351–3). Pandit Nehru's National Planning Committee agreed in 1938 that

The objective for the country as a whole was the attainment, as far as possible, of national self-sufficiency. International trade was certainly not excluded, but we were anxious to avoid being drawn into the whirlpool of economic imperialism. The first charge on the country's produce should be to meet the domestic needs of food, raw materials, and manufactured goods. Surplus production would not be dumped abroad but be used for exchange of such commodities as we might require. To base our national economy on export markets might lead to conflicts with other nations and to sudden upsets when those markets were closed to us. [Nehru 1946, p. 403]

The authors of *People's Plan* wanted post-independence India 'to exercise a monopolistic position in respect of foreign trade as well as financial transactions with foreign countries' (Banerjee *et al.* 1944, pp. 3–8). The desire to achieve self-sufficiency is also implicit in the Bombay Plan: 'We consider it essential for the success of our economic plan that the basic industries, on which ultimately the whole economic development of the country depends, should be developed as rapidly as possible . . . it should be our aim simultaneously to develop consumption goods industries so as to meet at least our essential requirements' (Thakurdas *et al.* pp. 31–2, 58).

With the establishment of the Planning Commission in 1950, and the formulation of successive five year development plans as frameworks for the centralized economic management of the economy, controls over agriculture, industry, foreign trade, and indeed economic decision-making by individuals and enterprises became the norm. The First Five Year Plan went so far as to claim that controls provide the appropriate incentive structure for rapid development:

Control and regulation of exports and imports, and in the case of select commodities state trading, are necessary not only from the point of view of utilizing to the best advantage the limited foreign exchange resources available but also for securing an allocation of the productive resources of the country in line with targets defined in the Plan . . . fiscal, monetary and commercial policy can influence the allocation of resources, but physical controls are also necessary . . . Viewed in the proper perspective, controls are but another aspect of the problem of incentives, for to the extent that controls limit the freedom of action on the part of certain classes, they provide correspondingly an incentive to certain others and the practical problem is always to balance the loss of satisfaction in one case against the gain in the other. *For one to ask for fuller employment and more rapid development and at the same time to object to controls is obviously to support two contradictory objectives.* [Planning Commission 1951, pp. 42–3, emphasis added]

In reality, the controls, largely in the form of various quantitative restrictions (QRs) and prohibitions, rather than in the form of taxes and subsidies (though these were also used, but often in conjunction with, rather than instead of, QRs and prohibitions) which operate through the market mechanism, ended up creating a chaotic incentive structure. They also encouraged and eventually unleashed rapacious rent seeking and political corruption, rather than the rapid development our planners claimed they would.

The consequences of the misguided state-controlled, public sector dominated, import-substituting industrialization with the emphasis on heavy industry are well known and well documented. As economic theory teaches us, restricting imports through tariffs and quotas, that is, explicit and implicit taxation of imports, is at the same time taxation of exports. In addition, our exchange rate remained overvalued for long periods of time. To offset the negative impacts on exports of import taxes and exchange rate overvaluation, various implicit and explicit measures of export subsidization were put in place. But access to some of them, such as duty drawbacks, were cumbersome, time-consuming, and corruption prone. The overall impact of export subsidization in offsetting the bias against exports, created by the import control regime, was at best modest and incomplete, and at worst negligible. While world exports grew at a rapid pace of 8 per cent per year from 1951 until the first oil shock of 1973 and at more modest rates (average rate of 2.6 per cent per year during 1973–85 and 5.7 per cent per year during 1985–96) thereafter, India's share in this growing world market dwindled from a high of 2.1 per cent in 1951 to a low of 0.4 per cent in 1980. It has climbed slowly since to about 0.6 per cent in 1997. Interestingly, China, whose share in world exports also declined in its pre-reform period from a high of 2.7 per cent in 1959 to a low of 0.7 per cent in 1977, has now regained what had been lost and gained some more. In 1997, China's share was 3.2 per cent (ibid.). The share of India's foreign trade in GDP remained virtually unchanged, around 12 per cent to 14 per cent of GDP during the four decades prior to the reforms of 1991.

Besides quantitative restrictions on imports there were tariffs as well, though clearly, with binding quotas, tariffs were not the effective constraints on imports.[1] The import weighted average of tariffs on all imports on the eve of reforms was 87 per cent, with the average for consumer goods being almost double at 164 per cent (World Bank 1998a, Annex Table 10). There was, of course, an enormous variance in tariffs across commodities, with rates on some imports exceeding 300 per cent. Given that tariffs on raw materials and capital goods were lower than on final goods, the rates of effective protection on some of the manufactured goods were extremely high. For example, imports of passenger automobiles were virtually banned on the ground that they were luxury goods. But this gave unlimited protection to the domestic manufactures. By controlling the price of this presumed luxury and rationing its available domestic output, the policy in effect transferred high rents to those who got the allocations, such as

---

[1] However it is possible that in the competition for import licences some might enter at lower tariffs but would drop it at higher rates. Also the composition of import demand would be affected by the structure of tariffs.

politicians and bureaucrats. The rationale of this policy by an ostensibly socialist regime was inexplicable, unless one believed that the rent transfer was indeed the intended outcome.

With respect to agriculture as a whole, as I discussed in Chapter 2, taking the explicit subsidies on some purchased inputs, such as fertilizers, the implicit taxes through export restrictions and other means and exchange rate overvaluation, the situation was one of disprotection on the average. Foreign trade in a number of agricultural commodities was canalized and the operation of the canalizing agencies was not exactly conducive to promote agricultural trade. Taking QRs and other non-tariff barriers into account, the coverage of non-tariff barriers was almost universal, around 90 to 95 per cent of trade prior to reform (World Bank 1998a, Annex Table 8).

I should also again refer to our policy of reservation of certain commodities for production by small scale enterprises. As stated in Chapter 1, the reservation of production of certain categories of cloth to handlooms together with import-substitution in machinery as well as restriction on technology imports in effect crippled our cotton textile mills, several of which became sick, then were taken over by the government, only to become more sick. Ironically a successful small enterprise had no incentive to grow beyond the size that would entitle it to receive government provided favours of all kinds as a small enterprise.

Given the harm that the control regime was doing to our growth and foreign trade, it is not surprising that Dr Manmohan Singh, who in his doctoral thesis at Oxford (later published as Singh 1964) had called attention to the crippling effect of India's trade policy and unwarranted export pessimism, would tackle the reform of the external trade regime as a priority. He abolished licensing and quantitative restrictions on most imports, except consumer goods. However, external trade in agricultural commodities was largely left out of his reform. Tariffs were reduced. By the time he left office in 1995, import weighted average tariffs on all imports had come down to 33 per cent from its level of 57 per cent in 1990-1. It has come down further to 30 per cent in 1998-9. The variance in tariffs had been reduced as well. Even consumer goods imports on an average had an import weighted tariff of 48 per cent in 1995, only 50 per cent higher than the overall average as compared to 100 per cent higher as it was in 1990–1. In 1998–9, the rate was 39 per cent, a third higher than the overall average. On agricultural products the weighted average tariffs were 70 per cent in 1990–1, 17 per cent in 1994–5, and 16 per cent in 1998–9 (World Bank 1998a, Annex Table 10). It is clear that since 1994–5 there has not been much further liberalization of tariffs.

The exchange rate is now by and large market determined, though it would be more accurate to say that we have a regime of managed, rather than cleanly floating, exchange rates. The real effective exchange rate had depreciated by about 48 per cent in 1995 relative to its value in 1990 (ibid., Annex Table 9). This depreciation, together with the reduction of import duties and restrictions, brought about a very modest increase in India's share of world exports from 0.53 per cent in 1990 to about 0.62 per cent in 1997 (ibid., Annex Table 7). With the slowing down of the reduction in tariffs since 1995, no change in non-tariff barriers, and some appreciation of the real effective exchange rate since 1995, it is not surprising that our export share has gone up only by 0.02 per cent to 0.62 per cent between 1995 and 1997 (ibid., Annex Table 7). In absolute terms, India's exports at $33 billion in 1998 were less than Thailand's post-crisis figure of $54 billion (IMF 1999, p. 64). In the last two years, export growth has slowed down considerably. The share of total trade (using data from the Department of Commercial Intelligence and Statistics) in GDP has, however, increased from 15.8 per cent in 1990–1 to 19.5 per cent in 1997–8 (Government of India 1999, Appendix Table 0.1). However, if we use the balance of payments data of the Reserve Bank, which report higher levels of exports and imports (particularly the latter), the share of trade in GDP goes up from 17.4 per cent in 1990–1 to 22.4 per cent in 1997–8 (ibid., Appendix Table 6.2).

Turning now to the present and the future, I will concentrate on areas directly related to foreign trade such as tariffs and non-tariff barriers, consumer goods imports, on integrating agriculture into the world markets, as well as on infrastructural bottlenecks on trade. In passing, let me say that we should liberalize trade with *all* our partners on a most favoured nation (MFN) basis rather than engage in preferential liberalization of our trade with our neighbours through the South Asian Preferential Trade Agreement (SAPTA). Of course, the untouched components of the reform agenda, such as labour and bankruptcy laws and the insurance sector, as well as unfinished items such as reform of the financial sector and privatization are also important from the perspective of foreign trade.

First, turning to consumer goods imports, as a signatory of the Uruguay Round Agreement we are committed to a phase-out of our quantitative restrictions. But our major trading partners filed a complaint against us in the World Trade Organisation (WTO) on the ground that our scheduled phase-out was too slow. We negotiated bilateral settlements on the pace of the phase-out with Australia, Canada, the European Union, Japan, New Zealand, and Switzerland. However, the US pursued its complaint and the WTO's Dispute Settlement Body (DSB) has ruled that we can no longer use the Balance of Payments (BOP) provision of GATT-WTO (Article XVIII B) for continuing with our quantitative restrictions. We have appealed against this ruling on the ground that the DSB has no jurisdiction for deciding whether the BOP provision could be invoked and only the BOP committee of the WTO can decide. The appeal is pending. In the meantime, tentative steps, by transferring around three hundred and fifty items from a list of restricted imports to the Open General Licence (OGL) categories have been taken, but many of these items are of limited significance. I would urge that we immediately convert the remaining QRs on consumer goods imports into tariffs and announce their reduction fairly rapidly.

I would also reduce our other tariffs, both in their levels and their variance. Compared to other developing countries in our region, our average and maximum tariffs are still high. Announcing a phased reduction would create more certainty for both domestic investors and FDI. It is very unfortunate that the Finance Minister, in his 1998–9 budget, announced an almost across the board additional tariff of 8 per cent (later reduced to 4 per cent) on all imports. This is an entirely wrong signal to send to the rest of the world if our intention in fact is to convey the idea that we have opened our economy significantly to foreign trade and investment. Bureaucratic and procedural hurdles faced by exporters and others are still formidable. The claim that all hurdles can now be cleared at one 'window' rather than from several windows separately will not do in a world where there are no hurdles at all to clear in many countries.

As pointed out in the previous chapters, our agricultural trade has yet to be freed from internal barriers, let alone be integrated with world markets. To repeat what I said, imports accounting for nearly three-fourths of the value of agricultural production are still subject to non-tariff barriers and quantitative restrictions on exports of most agricultural commodities still apply. I noted that India is still not a common market with taxes on interstate sales. Restrictions on interstate movement of agricultural commodities still exist. Restrictions on exports have often been imposed to moderate increases in domestic prices of politically sensitive commodities, for example, onions and raw cotton. There is massive government intervention in the market for cotton—for example, there is monopoly procurement in Maharashtra. Cotton export policy is driven by the consideration of keeping its price low for the textile industry.

I argued in Chapter 2 that full integration of agriculture with world markets and refraining from imposing restrictions on domestic trade is very likely to have significant once and for all price effects. But if we move, as we must, towards creating an efficient safety net for the truly poor, then its once and for all price effects need not come in the way of integration with world markets. Full integration also means that fluctuations in world prices of agricultural commodities will pass through to domestic prices. As stated earlier, this in fact will dampen domestic price fluctuations as compared to our current regime of insulating India's agriculture from world markets. I should also mention the fact that in some commodities, such as rice, the world trade is a small proportion of world output and, as such, any large trade by India could affect world prices. However, this is no reason for not trading, though we need to ensure that traders take into account the potential effect on world prices of their trade. The mechanism for bringing this about without violating WTO articles should be put in place.

I had drawn attention earlier to the forthcoming multilateral negotiations on agricultural trade in 2000. Let me emphasize that before entering these negotiations we should formulate our negotiating positions based on a rigorous analytical and empirical analysis of the issues involved. My impression is that in our participation in the Uruguay Round and earlier rounds, we took positions that were not thought through, based more on ideology than on our long term national interests, and opposed any trade liberalization. Because of this, I am told, the Indian delegate to GATT negotiations was named as Mr No by other delegates! Unfortunately some of the statements of the Commerce Minister, Mr Hegde, and the fact that not all delegates at the G–15 meeting of August 1999 in Bangalore shared our attitude towards a new round, suggest that the old mindset has not lost its hold.

My next set of remarks relate to infrastructural structural constraints on our foreign trade. The unreliability and poor quality of our power supply add to the costs of production of exportables and adversely affect our international competitiveness. Reforms of cargo handling at ports and road, rail, and air transportation to make them efficient and cost-effective are at an early stage. Also, to be able to break into the lucrative export markets for perishables, such as cut flowers, fresh fruits, and vegetables, we need an efficient cold storage, grading, and air transportation infrastructure.

Our policy with respect to private foreign capital of all types (foreign direct investment (FDI), portfolio investment, and debt) had been as restrictive, if not more, as the case of trade in goods and services before the 1991 reforms. Prior to 1991, restrictions on foreign direct investment included limits on entry into specified priority areas, an upper limit of 40 per cent on equity participation, and requirements on technology transfer, phased manufacturing, and export obligations. According to an estimate of Chopra *et. al.* (1995), government approvals for private investment were needed for 60 per cent of new investment in the industrial sector during the pre-1991 policy regime. They estimate that FDI averaged only around $200 million annually between 1985–91 with most of capital flows consisting of foreign aid, commercial borrowing, and deposits of non-resident Indians (NRIs).

The reforms of July 1991 affected FDI only to a limited extent. A discretionary mechanism of approval was introduced through the Foreign Investment Promotion Board (FIPB) for some industries. In addition, Indian firms with good standing have been allowed (since February 1992) to issue, with government approval, equity and convertible bonds abroad through the Global Depository Receipts (GDR) and American Depository Receipts (ADR) respectively in European and American capital markets.

Since September 1992, registered foreign institutional investors (FIIs) have also been permitted to purchase both equity and debt securities directly in the local market subject to certain upper limits.

As a consequence of the limited liberalization, FDI increased from $233 million in 1992 to an estimated $3.3 billion in 1997. India's share of total FDI in all developing countries increased from 0.5 per cent to 2.2 per cent over the same period. However, over this period China attracted massive flows of FDI amounting to $194.4 billion (cumulative) compared to $9.4 billion for India (Government of India 1999, p. 86). India's share in the total portfolio investment for all developing countries increased from 6.2 per cent in 1994 to 8.7 per cent in 1996 and declined to 5.1 per cent during 1997—the year of the East Asian currency crisis. Portfolio investment is volatile; fluctuations in the absolute amount of net flows were sharp: $5.3 billion in 1994, $1.4 billion in 1995, $4.6 billion in 1996, and $2.8 billion in 1997 (Government of India, p. 87).

Although government approved FDI proposals amounting to $54.3 billion during the eight-year period 1991–8, actual inflows were only $11.8 billion (cumulative) or a little over one-fifth of the approvals. A more disaggregated breakdown of the total FDI and portfolio investment over a seven-year period from 1990–1 to 1997–8 shows that India attracted a much larger magnitude of more volatile portfolio investment (cumulative $15.5 billion) than long-term FDI (cumulative $10.7 billion). Besides, two-thirds of FDI came through the non-transparent discretionary process of FIPB, 22 per cent from non-resident Indians, and only 11 per cent through the automatic route opened for private foreign investment in physical infrastructure in the July 1991 industrial policy. Private capital flows have indeed increased since 1991, but it is obvious that India has not attracted enough to finance the growing infrastructure investment requirements. The reason is also obvious: the old restrictive mindset with respect to foreign investment still prevails and liberalization has not been carried far enough. Equally, the limited liberalization resulting from the persistence of the old approach to foreign collaboration agreements can be gauged from some illustrative calculations of the World Bank. Of the 1,637 approvals granted during the two-year period 1988–9 and 1989–90 (under the pre-reform policy), as many as 888 or nearly 54 per cent would still have required government approval under the post-reform policy! India failed to share in the expansion of private capital flows in the 1990s. Developing countries as a group attracted foreign direct investment (FDI) flows of $29 billion per year on an average during 1986–91 (UNCTAD 1998). India had a share of 0.5 per cent of these flows compared to 12 per cent for China. FDI flows to developing countries increased nearly 4.5 times to $129.8 billion in 1996 and by more than 5 times to $148.9 billion in 1997. India increased its share to 1.8 per cent by 1996 but China's share rose to 31 per cent. The same report mentions that approvals of FDI in China have been going down and hence a short-term decline of FDI is to be expected in China. Given a receptive policy regime, there is plenty of room for India to expand its share of FDI flows. Much smaller countries like Thailand, Malaysia, and even Indonesia have received larger flows of FDI than India.

Postscript

The preceding eight chapters are obviously not comprehensive enough to cover all aspects of reform. I could also have delved more deeply than I did on those aspects that I covered. But the most serious of my omissions is a discussion of the politics or political economy of reforms.

My first visit to ISEC coincided with the general elections of 1998 that brought the BJP coalition to power. My lectures were delivered while the coalition had announced its first budget for the Union for the year 1998–9. I am writing this postscript in August 1999 after the fall of the coalition government while awaiting the polls for electing the next parliament to start in early September 1999. I would hope that the elections will bring to power a government at the Centre which will have a sufficient and stable majority in the Lok Sabha to be able to not only revive the reform agenda but to also deepen it and extend it. A different coalition led by BJP won an absolute majority and took oath of office in October 1999. The new government has announced its intention to acclerate reforms.

It is no exaggeration, but merely stating the obvious, if one were to say that not only the prospects of success of any reform agenda, but the scope, depth, sequencing, pace, and effectiveness of implementation of the agenda, which together influence the prospects of success, depend crucially on their political economy. The failures of several of our five year plans to achieve many of their targets, including, importantly, their aggregate growth targets, were attributed by some to their poor implementation, rather than to any faults in the formulation of the plans. But such an attribution reflects intellectual confusion—after all, any plan that had been formulated without taking into account the feasibility of its implementation is not a plan in any meaningful sense of the term. In the same vein, attributing the slowdown, if not altogether stalling, of the pace of our reforms to politics and lack of political will once again displays the same intellectual confusion. Put another way, a reform agenda not based on political realities but on wishful thinking, or worse still on myopic political calculations, is not a reform agenda but a recipe for frustration. This is not to say of course that political realities are either immutable or exogenous to the process of reform itself, but only to argue that the hallmark of farsighted and visionary political leadership is that it would mobilize the people by convincing them that reforms are in their interest. Only a myopic politician would surrender to the groups that have a vested interest in not reforming the system.

Roger Douglas, former Finance Minister of New Zealand, who was the architect of his country's successful structural reforms of 1984–95 (Evans *et al.* 1996), describes the conventional politics of reform very well:

. . . politicians tend, worldwide, to avoid structural reform until it is forced upon them by economic stagnation, a collapse of their currency, or some other economic and social disaster. Politicians tend to close their minds as long as they can to the need for structural reform, because they believe that decisive action must inevitably bring political calamity upon their governments.

As their countries' economies drift closer to crisis and structural problems are no longer deniable, they persuade themselves that action before the next election would give the advantage to their political opponents. [Douglas 1990, p. 2]

This could as well be a description of our own politicians. After all, it is the severe macroeconomic and balance of payments crisis of 1991 that brought India to a near default on her external debt and led to the Rao–Manmohan Singh reforms. The current slowdown of the reform process could be seen as illustrating Douglas' point that, incumbent politicians, particularly of a weak and unstable governing coalition such as ours at present, naturally would wish to postpone any decisive action that might conceivably erode their political support prior to the next election.

Douglas points out that

A fundamental choice is always there: You can take the costs upfront for larger medium-term gains, or focus on short-run satisfaction and be sandbagged later by the accumulated costs. There is a deep well of realism and common sense among the ordinary people of the community. They want politicians to have guts and vision to deliver sustainable gains in living standards. [ibid., p. 2]

This is well taken. While Prime Minister Rao and Dr Manmohan Singh indeed had the courage to realize the utter failure of the development strategy pursued until then and the need for systemic reforms and introduced them even though their party did not command an absolute majority in the parliament, unfortunately they did not try to mobilize public support for reforms. It is true that the crisis forced their hands with respect to the timing of announcement of reforms. But more could have been done to generate popular enthusiasm. In the absence of such an effort, like all the five year plans, the reforms appear to be more like 'top-down' impositions, than a consensus from a 'bottom-up' movement of ideas.

It is tragic that the Vajpayee government, while it did attempt to push the reform agenda further and faster, unfortunately chose to abandon our long-standing policy of creative ambiguity of our nuclear capability and resumed nuclear testing after a gap of twenty four years. Notwithstanding the hypocrisy of the five declared nuclear powers and the Chinese transfer of nuclear technology to Pakistan, our own security has been weakened rather than strengthened by the explosion and the proposed weaponization coupled with our declared 'no first use' policy. With respect to Pakistan, our security situation now is one of a balance of terror. With respect to China, our nuclear capability and 'no first use' are not credible policies since we do not have a convincing 'second strike' capability to retaliate and inflict sufficiently high damage if the Chinese were to attack us with nuclear weapons. In any case, the Chinese Communist leadership which did not hesitate to let thirty million people die in an avoidable famine not so long ago is unlikely to be deterred by the possibility that we might be able to destroy one or two of their cities. Those who naively point to the balance of nuclear terror between the NATO and Warsaw Pact nations as having prevented the cold war from escalating into a hot nuclear exchange forget that conventional wars with tragic consequences in Afghanistan,

Angola, and Vietnam were fought even while nuclear wars were eschewed. There is no reason to believe that the probability of a conflict with China or Pakistan using conventional arms has been reduced by the tests. Indeed the Kargil conflict with Pakistan is a demonstration of this fact and an even more ominous fact, namely that on both sides of the line of control extremists demanded its escalation to a nuclear confrontation. It must be said to the credit of the Vajpayee government that it showed tremendous restraint and ignored the clamours of the Sangh Parivar. Be that as it may, all that the testing has gained us is not greater security, but only international condemnation and economic sanctions by the US. In August 1999, a draft nuclear doctrine was announced—while confirming the 'no first use' policy, it stresses in effect a second strike capability by building a triad of delivery systems, land-based, air-based, and submarine-based. I am afraid that building a credible second-strike capability through such a triad would be very costly and in any case will trigger another arms race with Pakistan. Neither country can afford this madness.

If another unstable coalition comes to power, it is very unlikely that the reform process will be accelerated any time soon. On the other hand, if the BJP comes to power with a majority, and succumbs to the demands of Swadeshi Jagaran Manch, it would send the economy back to the failed era of import-substitution. Even if this dire eventuality does not materialize but no further reforms take place, infrastructural constraints would become more severe, fiscal deficits would crowd out productive investment, export potential would remain underutilized, and our growth rate would regress back towards the contemporary Hindu growth rate, that is a rate adjusted for the changes in the sectoral composition of GDP since the 1950s, of 5 per cent per year. Fortunately, the election manifestos of the BJP-led National Democratic Alliance and the Congress Party promise fiscal prudence (through the enactment of a Fiscal Responsibility Act) and recognize the need for FDI (particularly in the infrastructural sectors) and for faster export growth. Unfortunately neither manifesto seriously addresses privatization, labour market, and bankruptcy reforms. As noted earlier the National Democratic Alliance won an absolute majority and it has promised to accelerate reforms.

There is one slight glimmer of hope in this gloomy scenario, namely that weakness and instability at the centre might lead some states to be bolder and more imaginative in introducing reforms and their success would lead other states to emulate them. I certainly hope that I am proved wrong in my pessimism. If I am proved right, we would once again have let down our poor masses. It would be indeed unconscionable if the realistic possibility of rapid growth and poverty alleviation is sacrificed at the altar of jingoistic and myopic politics.

The government that comes to power after the September 1999 elections, whether stable or not, reform-minded or not, has to face the fact that the third ministerial meeting of the WTO will convene in Seattle, USA in late November 1999. It is expected that the meeting will launch another round of multilateral negotiations. Whether it is launched or not, the TRIPS and Agriculture agreements will come up for review in 2000 as a part of the built-in agenda of the Uruguay Round. In addition, as yet there is no agreement on movement of natural persons. Negotiations on this and on the Maritime Services component of General Agreement on Trade in Services (GATS) are also to take place in the same year. It is essential that the new government develop our negotiating positions after careful thought. Let me conclude with a few remarks on my view of what India should ask for in these negotiations.

India has a vital interest in ensuring that any agreement reached on movement of natural persons is very liberal. India is likely to have comparative advantage in labour-intensive services as well as in certain skill-intensive ones such as software. The software industry is one of India's fastest growing industries in the electronics sector. Software exports grew by an impressive 43 per cent per year between 1991–2 and 1996–7 and 68 per cent in 1997–8. Although India's share in the world software market has been low, in customized software India's recent share is a commanding 16 per cent. In the Silicon Valley of California

Almost 3000 of the region's high tech companies are run by Chinese and Indian engineers . . . Apart from generating annual sales of almost $17 bn last year and providing 58,000 jobs in California's high-tech zone, Asian entrepreneurs have established long-distance business networks especially with Taiwan and India, which offer valuable openings for investment and trade . . . . Chinese and Indian chief executives ran 13 per cent of the Silicon Valley technology companies started between 1980 and 1984 and 29 per cent of those launched between 1995 and 1998. [*Financial Times,* 3–4 July 1999, p. 3]

While exports of software from a domestic base will continue to grow, to be able to provide *in situ* services in foreign markets and to keep up with technological developments it is essential that Indian software technicians have the opportunity to work abroad without necessarily having to migrate permanently. Most of the Indian engineers entered the United States under a special category of non-immigrant visas but there is strong pressure to restrict the number of such visas issued. A liberal agreement on movement of natural person would facilitate such temporary migration.

Reminiscent of its resistance to the start of the Uruguay Round of multilateral trade negotiations, India is again reluctant to endorse the start of a new 'millennium' round on the grounds, among others, that developed countries have not lived up to their commitments in earlier rounds. This reluctance is unfortunate. First of all, if the major trading powers of the world are for it, there is nothing India or the developing countries, which together do not account for a significant share of world trade, could do to stop it. Winham (1989, p. 54) attributed to one official who was involved in the negotiations that led to the Uruguay Round the following description of those negotiations: 'It was a brutal but salutary demonstration that power would be served in that nations comprising five percent of world trade were not able to stop negotiation sought by nations comprising ninety-five per cent of world trade.' Second, there are several reasons why it is in India's interest to ensure an early launch and successful completion of the Millennium Round. Bergsten (1999) lists many of them and also identifies several issues that are of great interest to India and which, in his view, India could present in the new round:

1. Elimination of the high tariffs that will remain, especially in the United States, on many Indian apparel and textile exports after the phase-out of quotas under the MFA;
2. Elimination of the very high tariffs on agricultural imports in many industrialized countries, especially on products of export interest to India (such as rice);

3. New agreements on foreign direct investment that would both expand its levels and help India achieve a fair share of its benefits, as described above;
4. Tougher disciplines on the use of anti-dumping duties, especially by the United States and the European Union;
5. Liberalization of movement of natural persons, where India has a strong competitive advantage, under the General Agreement on Trade in Services;
6. Elimination of preferential tariffs in regional arrangements, including the EU and NAFTA, that discriminate against Indian exports; and
7. Further straightening of the DSM to help protect the rights of countries with smaller trade levels.

I would, however, strengthen a few of Bergsten's suggestions and add some of my own. The European Commission had recommended the imposition of anti-dumping (ADM) duties on gray cotton cloth exports of India and a few other countries, a recommendation that could be attributed only to crass protectionist motives. Fortunately the Council of Ministers rejected this recommendation. Unless checked, the use of ADMs to circumvent or evade liberalization commitments will grow. Rather than attempt to toughen the disciplines on the use of ADMs, I would suggest that India and other developing countries should take the lead in pushing for the abolition of their use altogether. In my view, ADMs are the analogues of chemical and biological weapons in the arsenal of trade policy instruments. Unfortunately India has begun to emulate the worst practices of the industrialized countries by becoming the third or fourth most frequent user of ADMs in 1998. I strongly deplore this.

Also, rather than ask for elimination of preferential tariffs against Indian exports in regional and preferential trade agreements (PTAs) of which India is not a member, we would go further and suggest that India should push for replacing Article XXIV of GATT dealing with Customs Unions and Free Trade Areas, with the requirement that preferences granted to partners in any PTA should be extended on a MFN basis to all members of the WTO within a specified period, say five to ten years. Here again India, like many other developing countries, is moving in the wrong direction of championing regional agreements such as South Asian Preferential Trade Agreement (SAPTA) and also clamouring to become a member of other regional agreements. In my judgment, the discriminatory and trade-diverting aspects of PTAs, regardless of whether they are 'open' or not, far outweigh any benefits to be reaped. In fact, Open Regionalism is almost an oxymoron—either a trading arrangement is open in the only relevant sense, viz. it does not discriminate among trading partners or it is regional and discriminates against non-members outside the region. It cannot be both.

It was a mistake to have included TRIPS in the mandate of the WTO. If India and other developing countries are not vigilant, it is possible that the use of trade sanctions for enforcing non-trade-related objectives such as human rights, labour, and environmental standards would become legitimized through the expansion of WTO's mandate. Thus far, at the first two ministerial meetings of WTO in Singapore (1996) and Geneva (1998), the ministers have firmly shut the door against a social clause in the WTO. But the future is unclear. The inability of members of the WTO to arrive at a consensus on a candidate to replace Mr. Renato Ruggiero, whose term as Director General of WTO expired on 30 April 1999, was in part related to the desire of some industrialized countries to replace him with one of the two candidates who are viewed as more sympathetic to the inclusion of a social clause and the opposition of developing countries as well as some industrialized countries to such a choice. Now that the members of WTO have decided on a compromise that both candidates will share a six year term, it is to be hoped that the struggle that occurred before the compromise was reached does not weaken the organization. Be that as it may, developing countries, including India and the sympathetic developed countries, should ensure that in any future round of trade negotiations labour standards issues are forever kept out of the WTO.

References

Bannerjee, B. M. *et al.* (1944), *People's Plan for Economic Development of India* (Bombay: Indian Federation of Labour).

Basu, D. D. (1994), *Introduction to the Constitution of India* (New Delhi: Prentice Hall).

Bergsten, F. (1999), 'India and the Global Trading System', Annual Commencement Day Lecture at the Export-Import Bank of India, Mumbai, 10 March (processed).

Bhagwati, J. (1998), 'Review of Joshi and Little (1996) and Drèze and Sen (1995)', *Economic Journal,* Vol. 107, January, pp. 196–200.

Brecher, R. and C. Alejandro (1977), 'Tariffs, Foreign Capital and Immiserizing Growth', *Journal of International Economics,* Vol. 7, pp. 317–22.

Buiter, W. and U. Patel (1992), 'Debt, Deficits and Inflation: An Application to the Public Finances of India', *Journal of Public Economics,* Vol. 47, pp. 171–205.

_____ (1996), 'Solvency and Fiscal Correction in India: An Analytical Discussion', in S. Mundle (ed.), *Fiscal Policy in India,* (New Delhi: Oxford University Press).

_____ (1997), 'Budgetary Aspects of Stabilization and Structural Adjustment', in M. Blejer and T. Ter-Minassian (eds), *Macroeconomic Dimensions of Public Finance: Essays in Honour of Vito Tanzi,* (London and New York: Routledge), pp. 363–412.

Burgess, R., S. Howes, and N. Stern, (1993), 'The Reform of Indirect Taxes in India', Economic Transformation and Public Finance Discussion Paper EF7, London School of Economics, November, 1993.

Burgess, R. and N. Stern (1993), 'Tax Reform in India', Suntory–Toyota International Centre for Economics and Related Disciplines, London School of Economics, Discussion Paper No. 45 (processed).

_____ (1994), 'Reform of Domestic Trade Taxes in India: Issues and Options', (New Delhi: National Institute of Public Finance and Policy) (processed).

Chopra, A., C. Collyns, R. Hemming, and K. Parker with W. Chu and O. Fratzscher (1995), 'India: Economic Reforms and Growth', IMF Occasional Paper No. 134.

Demery, L. and M. Walton (1998), 'Are Poverty and Social Goals for the 21st Century Attainable?', World Bank (processed).

Department of Fertilizers (1998), *Fertilizer Pricing Policy*, Ministry of Chemicals and Fertilizers, Government of India.

Diaz-Alejandro, C. (1985), 'Good-Bye Financial Repression, Hello Financial Crash', *Journal of Development Economics*, Vol. 19, pp. 1–24.

Douglas, R. (1990), 'The Politics of Successful Structural Reform', *Policy*, Vol. 6, No. 1, Autumn, pp. 2–6.

Drèze, Jean and A. Sen (1995), *India Economic Development and Social Opportunity*, (Oxford: Clarendon Press).

Evans, L., A. Grimes, and B. Wilkinson with David Teece (1996), 'Economic Reform in New Zealand 1984-95: The Pursuit of Efficiency', *The Journal of Economic Literature*, Vol. 34, No. 4, December, pp. 1856–1902.

Gopal, S. (1984), *Selected Works of Jawaharlal Nehru*, (New Delhi: Jawaharlal Nehru Memorial Fund).

Government of India (1999), *Economic Survey 1998–1999*, (New Delhi: Government of India Press).

_____ (1998), *Economic Survey 1997–98*, (New Delhi: Government of India Press).

_____ (1997), *Government Subsidies in India*, (New Delhi: Ministry of Finance).

IMF (1999), *International Financial Statistics*, Volume LII, Number 6, June, (Washington DC: International Monetary Fund).

Joshi, V. and I. Little (1996a), *India's Economic Reforms 1991–2001*, pp. 171–94 (Oxford: Clarendon Press).

_____ (1996b), 'Macroeconomic Management in India, 1964–1994', in V. Balasubramaniam and D. Greenaway, *Trade and Development: Essays in honour of J. N. Bhagwati* (London: Macmillan).

_____ (1994), *India: Macroeconomics and Political Economy 1964–1991* (Washington, DC: The World Bank).

Joskow, P. (1999), 'Regulatory Priorities for Reforming Infrastructure Sectors in Developing Countries', in J. Stiglitz and B. Pleskovic (eds.), *Annual Bank Conference on Development Economics 1998*, pp. 191–233 (Washington, DC: World Bank).

Kangle, R. P. (1972), *The Kautilāya Arthaśāstra, Part II*, (Bombay: University of Bombay).

Mahalanobis, P. C. (1969), 'The Asian Drama: An Indian View', *Sankhya: The Indian Journal of Statistics*, Series B, Vol. 31, Parts 3 & 4.

_____ (1961), *Talks on Planning*, Indian Statistical Series No. 14, (Calcutta: Statistical Publishing Society).

McKinnon, R. (1973), *Money and Capital in Economic Development*, (Washington, DC: Brookings Institution).

Ministry of Finance (1992), *Final Report of the Tax Reforms Committee*, (New Delhi: Ministry of Finance).

Murdock, K. and J. E. Stiglitz (1993), 'The Effects of Financial Repression in an Economy with Positive Real Rates', Background Paper for World Bank, East Asian Miracle, (Washington, DC: World Bank).

Naoroji, D. (1901), *Poverty and Un-British Rule in India*, (New York: Swan and Sonnerschein).

Nehru, Jawaharlal (1946), *The Discovery of India*, (New York: The John Day Company).

Parikh, K.S., G. Fischer, K. Frohb, and O. Gulbrandsen (1988), *Towards Free Trade in Agriculture*, (Dordrecht: Martinus Nijhoff Publishers).

Peters, H. (1997), 'Reforming India's Port System: A Position Paper', presented at Japan Chamber of Commerce and the World Bank, Follow-up Workshop on the Power and Transportation Sectors: India, Tokyo, 14 May 1997.

Planning Commission (1951), *The First Five Year Plan*, (New Delhi: Government Printing Office).

Radhakrishna, R. and K. Subbarao (1997), 'India's Public Distribution System', Discussion Paper No. 380, (Washington, DC: World Bank).

Shaw, E. (1973), *Financial Deepening in Economic Development*, (New York: Oxford University Press).

Singh, M. (1964), *India's Export Trends*, (Oxford: Clarendon Press).

Srinivasan (1998), 'India's Export Performance: A Comparative Analysis', in I. J. Ahluwalia and I. M. D. Little (eds), *India's Economic Reforms and Development: Essays for Manmohan Singh*, (Delhi: Oxford University Press).

_____ (1992), 'Planning and Foreign Trade Reconsidered', in S. Roy and W. E. James (eds), *Foundations of India's Political Economy: Towards an Agenda for the 1990s*, (New Delhi: Sage Publications).

Srinivasan, T. N. and P. Bardhan (1974), *Poverty and Income Distribution in India*, (Calcutta: Statistical Publishing Society).

Stiglitz, J. (1994), 'The Role of the State in Financial Markets', in *Proceedings of the World Bank Annual Conference on Development Economics 1993*, Supplement to the *World Bank Economic Review*.

Thakurdas, P. *et al.* (1944), *A Plan of Economic Development of India*, (London: Penguin Books).

UNCTAD (1998), *World Investment Report*, Geneva.

Visveswaraya, Sir M. (1934), *Planned Economy for India,* (Bangalore: Bangalore Press).

Williamson, J. and M. Mahar (1998), 'A Review of Financial Liberalization', *Princeton Essay in International Finance,* No. 211.

Winham, G. (1989), 'The Prenegotiation Phase of the Uruguay Round', in Janice Gross Stein (ed.), *Getting to the Table,* (Baltimore and London: Johns Hopkins University Press), pp. 44–67.

World Bank (1998a), *India: 1998 Macro-Economic Update,* (Washington, DC: World Bank).

_____ (1998b), *India: Reducing Poverty in India,* Report No. 17881-IN (Washington, DC: World Bank).

_____ (1996), *India: Country Economic Memorandum,* Report No. 15882-IN (Washington, DC: World Bank).

_____ (1997), *India: 1997 Economic Update: Sustaining Rapid Growth,* Report No. 16506-IN (Washington, DC: World Bank).

Author Index

Subject Index